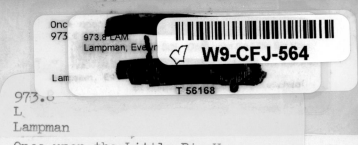

DATE DUE

MAR 3 0 2015			

DISCARD

Demco

Once upon the Little Big Horn

Once upon

Custer

Lt. Varnum

Sitting Bull

he Little Big Horn

By Evelyn Sibley Lampman
Illustrated by John Gretzer

Thomas Y. Crowell Company
New York

Gall

Crazy Horse

nesome Charley

Cpt. Benteen

Designed by Carole Halpert

Manufactured in the United States of America

L.C. Card 78–113855
ISBN 0-690-59540-9

1   2   3   4   5   6   7   8   9   10

When the white man wins it is a battle. When the Indian wins it is a massacre.

—Old Indian Saying

Once upon the Little Big Horn

JUNE 24, 1876, evening

When his second wife informed him that the evening meal was ready, Sitting Bull came outside and sat in the shade cast by the buffalo hides stretched over the conical lodge poles. It was still very hot, and he wished that tonight's social dances had not required that he don his full regalia. Sitting Bull had always been indifferent to clothes, and dressing the role was for him the most difficult part of being head chief of the Sioux.

On his head was a magnificent war bonnet with a tail of eagle feathers that trailed to the ground. Each feather represented a brave deed performed in the past, and because Sitting Bull was a very brave man, the tail was double, with feathers on either side. It was supported by a beaded browband with dangling ermine pendants, which felt close and sticky on his perspiring forehead.

He was also required to wear the deerskin shirt of the Midnight Strong Hearts, of which he was the leader. It was decorated with porcupine quills, beads, and human hair, stained red and yellow, and on one shoulder was painted a red cross, signifying that he had killed a Crow chief after he himself had been seriously wounded in battle. The long fringed sleeves were especially uncomfortable tonight, since Sitting Bull was recovering from the torture of a recent Sun Dance, during which he had given a hundred pieces of skin from his arms to *Wakan Tanka,* the Great Mystery.

The hundred scabs, fifty on each arm, were still sensitive to the touch, and the flesh around them red and swollen, but the sacrifice had been worthwhile. *Wakan Tanka* had rewarded him with a vision of white soldiers falling head first into camp. It meant that soon there would be a battle, and that the Sioux and their allies would be victorious.

As Sitting Bull squatted on the ground, one of his two wives handed him a great spoon made of horn, filled with the fragrant stew which had been cooking over the fire.

Sitting Bull took a satisfying mouthful. It was delicious. Young puppy, he decided, probably the one that couldn't be broken from its barking.

Dogs were a necessity of life, and the camp was

overflowing with them. They came in every size and shape, and in color ranged from pure black to grayish brown. With their sharp faces and pointed ears, they all bore a slight resemblance to that wisest of animals, the coyote. The big dogs were used to pull travois, and the small ones were for eating, but even a large dog that barked too much would end up in the stew pot. A barking dog might give away the location of the camp to the enemy.

Sitting Bull's first wife came to stand beside him while he ate. With his eagle-wing fan, she brushed away the hungry flies that wished to share his meal.

He gave her a friendly smile of appreciation. Usually Sioux warriors took the unending services of women for granted, but Sitting Bull was different. He was kind to everyone, with a jolly word or a joke to make people laugh, and he was never haughty or arrogant. These were the qualities that had led to his selection as the first principal chief of all the Sioux.

The members of the Sioux nation had not chosen their head chief because he was the greatest warrior. They had chosen him because he was good-hearted and generous, and above personal spite and selfishness. He also had the gift of prophecy and was able to make strong prayers; he was a good singer of many songs and had the ability to hold people together.

Sitting Bull also had great cunning and shrewdness. His appointments of subordinates had been wisely made: Gall, as his war chief, and the Midnight Strong Hearts to enforce the rules of the camp. With their help he had been able to hold the Sioux hunting grounds against enemy tribes and to gain new ones. Now he was gathering together the greatest collection of Plains Indians the country had ever seen.

They had united for mutual protection against their common enemy, the white man, who was trying to steal their lands and force the Indians to live like fenced-in cattle on small plots called reservations. And they were coming together in answer to the summons of their head chief, Sitting Bull.

The several tribes of Sioux had been united for only two summers. During their first council, they had elected Sitting Bull of the Hunkpapa Sioux head chief, with Crazy Horse of the True Oglala as his second in command. There had been only one dissenting voice, that of Spotted Tail of the Brulé who wanted the honor for himself. The other tribes remembered how the Hunkpapa had flourished under Sitting Bull; how when the buffalo was scarce, he had led war parties into the lands of the Shoshone, the Crow, and the Ree, winning new hunting grounds for his people; how he had eluded the white soldiers and closed his ears to the demands of the Grandfather in Washington; how *Wakan Tanka* had favored him with many visions and with prophecies come true. These were all things needful in a head chief.

"When you say fight, we will fight. When you say peace, we will make peace," pledged the Hunkpapa, the Miniconjou, the Sans Arc, the Yanktonai, the Two Kettle, and the Blackfeet Sioux. And after they left the council, each tribe for its own preserve, they remembered.

Now they were coming back. Sitting Bull had sent out runners, and the Sioux had opened their ears. The Hunkpapa circle of lodges was but one of seven circles of council fires, each circle representing a tribe of Sioux or Cheyenne. Their lodges extended over three miles along the southern bank of the Greasy Grass, which the whites called the Little Big Horn River. It was impossible to see from one end of the encampment to the other, and while no one had ever counted, there were probably ten thousand Indians here and more ar-

riving every day. Sitting Bull's heart grew strong
at the thought.

He licked the last of the stew from the horn
spoon and handed it to his first wife to refill at the
cooking fire.

Some of the Sioux had not waited for his call,
Sitting Bull remembered. Many had joined on
their own initiative. These were smaller groups
who trembled to live alone. It was no longer safe
as in the old days. The white man was making it
more and more difficult.

The whites laid strips of iron for a road straight

through the best hunting preserves. They strung wire between tall poles, and the wire was magic, for it could carry the words of man from one spot to a distant place and this more quickly than a pony could run. Their oxen and horses ate the grass, and they drove off and killed the game. They brought sickness, and the winds carried it to the Indians, and thousands died.

Soldiers arrived to build forts, which they said were to protect them from the Indians, and they sent word that the Indians must live on the land surrounding the forts, called reservations. Some of the tribes, weakened by war and sickness, agreed. They folded their tepees and meekly moved to this confinement where they were doled out small amounts of poor food and cheap supplies with each new moon. However, they did not conform exactly as the whites hoped, for they did not spread out on their reservation land. They clustered their lodges closely around the walls of the fort and the agency store. It was easier to receive their gifts in this way, but it earned for them the name of agency Indians. The very thought brought a scornful curl to Sitting Bull's lips.

Of the Sioux, only Red Cloud and his three hundred Bad-Face-Oglala and the Brulé under Spotted Tail, who still rankled over the selection of Sitting Bull as chief, had touched the peace paper. Red Cloud's action had caused a split in the Oglala, for Crazy Horse had spurned the white man's paper. Followed by thirty of his tribesmen, he had come to join Sitting Bull, because there were too few of them to survive alone.

Sitting Bull had been glad to welcome them. As head chief of the Sioux, he was responsible for the welfare of all his people, and he had great respect for the True Oglala who refused to live on the reservation. Although some of his young men occasionally rode into an agency to jeer, Sitting Bull himself had never set foot in one. He wanted no presents from the Grandfather in Washington, and he would not touch a pen to the peace paper to give away the land of *Wakan Tanka*. The Great Mystery had given the Indians the right to live on the land and hunt the game, but he had not given them the right to dispose of it.

One day some white soldiers, led by the officer Long Hair, had discovered gold in *Pa Sapa,* the sacred hills of the Sioux nation. The tribes had been aware of the yellow metal, but had kept silent, knowing how it was cherished by the whites. Now the country was filled with men who had come to defile the holy place and dig in the sacred earth. Even the Indians who lived on the reservations were angry, but their protests fell on closed ears.

The miners killed Indians whenever they could, so the Sioux killed miners in return. The soldiers, who had killed before, particularly when they were filled with the fiery water called whiskey, killed even more, nor were they always particular to distinguish between friends and enemies. They looked only for a red skin.

Sitting Bull's heart had swollen large with anger when he heard the stories, nor had he been alone in those feelings. The lodges under his direct command had increased to fifteen hundred as tribesmen came from small bands to unite with his. They had to be constantly on the move to find food for so many.

The last winter, spent in the Blue Mountains in the west, had been very hard on them, Sitting Bull thought sadly. He raised his eyes from the horn spoon to look around the Hunkpapa circle. Some of the lodges were missing, destroyed as was the custom on the death of their owners. Not all had belonged to old men with teeth too loose to chew the diet of dried meat. Some were those of young braves, the best hunters, who had ventured out in snowshoes over glare ice in search of fresh game. They had never returned, as they would

have done had they not met death. But most of
the Sioux had survived, and when spring came, it
brought the Cheyenne.

Sitting Bull had welcomed them warmly. The
Cheyenne were among the fiercest fighters on the
plains and had long been allies of the Sioux. He
had brought the chiefs into his own lodge, given
them food, and afterward, when the pipe passed
around, they had told their story.

In the Moon of Snow Blindness, when winter drew to an end, a sleeping Cheyenne village had been attacked by soldiers. The soldiers had captured the camp, burned all of the 120 lodges, and driven away the pony herd. Many defenseless women and children had been left dead on the snow, the way whites liked to do.

The Cheyenne had awaited their chance, then stolen back their ponies, and with angry hearts set out to find Sitting Bull wintering in the Blue Mountains. They had heard that he was uniting the Sioux, and they wished to join their forces with his. If there was to be a fight with the white soldiers, the Cheyenne were ready to avenge their dead.

Sitting Bull had been glad to have these fierce warriors, and their story hardened his heart to iron. So far the Sioux had skillfully eluded a direct battle with the whites, and contented themselves with small raids against miners and settlers. Now the time for running away had come to an end. The Indians would have to fight to protect their own.

He had sent runners in all directions, to every camp of hunting bands, to every reservation west of the Missouri.

"It is war," said the messengers. "Sitting Bull is traveling to the valley of the Rosebud. Join him there at the river's bend. Together we will make one big fight with the soldiers. We will settle this for all time."

Then Sitting Bull had given orders to break camp, and the Sioux and Cheyenne began moving slowly toward the rendezvous, pausing often to fill their stomachs with fresh game and the early roots dug by the women. There was no hurry. It was then late spring, the Moon of Shedding Ponies. It would take time for the runners to reach their destinations, but by the next moon, the Moon for Making Fat, all should be assembled.

As soon as they heard, the tribes answered the call. Lame Deer had led his Miniconjou to the Rosebud and repledged his allegiance to the head chief. With them came that great warrior High Backbone, called Hump, whose coups and deeds were legendary on the plains. Then came the Sans Arc under Spotted Eagle, and the Blackfeet Sioux, so called because their women stained the skins of their moccasins black. There were also some Yanktonai, some Cuthead and Two Kettle Sioux scattered through the camps, and a few tribesmen from the Arapaho and some Santee under their warrior chief Inkpaduta, who wished to join the Sioux in a battle against the whites. When there were not enough members of a single tribe to make a circle of their own, they were welcomed into other groups.

The runners had gone also to the reservations of Red Cloud and Spotted Tail, and all the restless young men opened their ears. They sharpened their knives, traded for guns and ammunition, and as soon as the grass was high and their ponies fat, they too headed for the Rosebud. The agency chiefs could not hold them. Even Red Cloud's son, Jack Red Cloud, had closed his ears to his father's words and ridden away.

Reservation life had not lived up to the promises made for it. There was nothing to do but sit and stare at the outer walls of the fort. For small infractions of rules, men were thrown into the stockade and penned up like animals. There was not enough to eat, and their bellies were always empty. They were tired of the Grandfather's unfulfilled promises and worthless presents, of flour that was filled with weevils, sugar mixed with sand, thin blankets so small one would not cover a man, and pants that fell apart after the first wearing.

So many Brulé had deserted Spotted Tail that they formed their own council fire. The Oglala circle under Crazy Horse had grown to over seventy lodges, with an uncounted number of wickiups which sheltered young braves without families.

Crazy Horse, encouraged by the growing numbers, had advised attacking each of the forts in turn, driving the whites from the country by force, but Sitting Bull was more cautious.

First, he had insisted, he must make medicine. He would ask *Wakan Tanka* for a vision. Even though it was not July, the Moon of Cherries' Ripening, the usual time for the Sun Dance, he would make a special one. He would give *Wakan Tanka a* scarlet blanket, his own blood, and ask the Great Mystery for advice. The young men, yearning for a fight, had grown silent then. They knew there was wisdom in the words.

It was now nearly half a moon since Sitting Bull had made the dance. He had suffered stoically while the hundred pieces of skin were cut from his arms; then all the remainder of that day he danced, with his eyes fixed on the blazing sun. He danced all night and until noon of the following day, when he had fallen to the earth as though dead.

"I give you these because they have no ears." *Wakan Tanka*'s voice had come to him in a dream. And Sitting Bull had seen white soldiers, who would not listen to caution, come falling into the Sioux camp like grasshoppers, with their hats dropping to the ground.

It had been a true vision, and meant that *Wakan*

Tanka would defend the side of right. All the people rejoiced.

Because game was growing scarce on the Rosebud, they had moved on into the next valley, the valley of the Little Big Horn. There, while the Sioux were camped on the Creek of Many Ash Trees, the scouts through flashing hand mirrors had reported that the valley of the Rosebud behind them was black with soldiers. It had been a great war party: 1000 soldiers and 250 scouts—Ree, Shoshone, and Crow—under Gray Fox, the white man General Crook.

Led by Crazy Horse, the Sioux and Cheyenne warriors had set out to do battle with their enemy. Sitting Bull had gone, also, but his wounds from the Sun Dance had been too recent for him to take any part except that of onlooker.

Behind a high hill on the west bank of the Rosebud, they had halted to rest their ponies and prepare for battle. Each warrior put on his finest clothing, for if he should be killed, the enemy on seeing his body would know he had been a man of consequence. They painted their faces carefully, some using the zigzag streaks of lightning, for thunder is a powerful medicine. Sacred dust was strewn on their ponies to make them fleet and

invincible, and each man checked his weapons. Then they waited.

They had hoped to draw the soldiers into a trap and close the retreat, but the soldiers would not be drawn. The battle had been almost a free-for-all, each side charging back and forth with neither gaining an advantage. Finally the soldiers began withdrawing, and the Sioux and Cheyenne were left with the field.

The warriors were well pleased. It had been a good fight. Only thirteen of the tribesmen had been killed and a number wounded, with an equal number of casualties among the white soldiers. They had used up most of their ammunition, which was a bad thing because ammunition was hard to find, but Gray Fox had taken his soldiers and gone away, so the Indians counted it a victory.

But it wasn't the fulfillment of *Wakan Tanka*'s prophecy. These soldiers had been intercepted. They had not fallen into camp. There was another battle still to come, Sitting Bull had insisted.

He thought about that battle now as he sat before his lodge, chewing on the puppy stew flavored with wild onion and turnips. It would be a great battle when it came, perhaps the most important battle in which the Sioux had ever been engaged. But he was not worried. *Wakan Tanka* was watching over his people, and *Wakan Tanka* had promised victory.

Sitting Bull finished his meal and rose stiffly to his feet. An old battle injury had left him crippled in one leg, and he walked with a noticeable limp. He motioned to his wives to raise the sides of his lodge to let in the air. Then he entered and sat down to await his visitors.

On nights of social dancing there were many visitors—young bucks from other tribes who came to dance with the maidens, and chieftains who might call to pay their respects to Sitting Bull. He was getting a little tired of social dances, but it would have been discourteous not to celebrate the arrival of those who had traveled far. Since new groups rode in almost every day, it was a rare evening when Sitting Bull was not required to don garments appropriate to the head chief of the Sioux.

His first caller this evening was Crazy Horse. Crazy Horse was younger than Sitting Bull, and he had a pale skin and light hair that matched the color of the weasel-fur wrappings around his long braids. A long powder-darkened scar crossed one cheek from his nose to his jawbone, and his face was painted with the white circles favored by the Oglala.

ONCE UPON THE LITTLE BIG HORN   22

Like Sitting Bull, Crazy Horse scorned finery of any kind, and even though he was second in command, he refused to wear it. Tonight he was dressed in his usual clothes—a white buckskin shirt, blue leggings, and a single feather at the back of his head.

Sitting Bull rose to meet his visitor, courteously ushering him from left to right into the lodge. The guest was given the place of honor, next to the head chief himself, on the skin-covered bed at the rear.

Before Sitting Bull finished filling the long stone pipe with tobacco mixed with red willow, the second visitor arrived. This was Two Moon of the Cheyenne, stocky, dark-skinned, with a wide mouth that seemed to run from one ear to the other.

In the circle made by the Hunkpapa lodges, the dancing had begun, and as the pipe passed from hand to hand, the sounds of drums, of singing and merrymaking, came to the three men seated upon the fur robes.

At length Two Moon reported the news that had brought him from one end of the encampment to the other. Earlier that day one of the Cheyenne holy men had stood on the banks of the Greasy Grass and howled like a wolf. Immediately his cry had

been answered by a real wolf on the opposite bank, and this he interpreted to mean that here would be the site of a new battle. Before long there would be plenty of dead meat on the ground to feed the wolves.

Sitting Bull nodded, smiling. It only bore out his vision, he reminded them. There would be soldiers falling into camp very soon.

Both Crazy Horse and Two Moon respected Sitting Bull's prophecies. He had made many, and they had always come true.

Two Moon pointed out that the prophecy would have to be fulfilled very soon. The plan was to camp but one sleep more on the Greasy Grass. With so many people and such a great herd of ponies, it was impossible to stay very long in one place. As the game and the grass were exhausted, they had to move on. The holy man had interpreted the wolf as meaning that the battle would be here, on the Greasy Grass, and that must mean that it would be tomorrow.

Sitting Bull nodded again. The scouts were out. They had reported that pony soldiers (cavalry) were once again in the next valley, the valley of the Rosebud, but as yet they were too far away for alarm. When the soldiers came, they would be as grasshoppers falling into camp. The Sioux and Cheyenne need not go out seeking war. It would come to them.

General George Armstrong Custer handed the reins of his thoroughbred to his hostler and stretched to his full six feet, easing the tired muscles of his long legs.

Before him the officers and men of the Seventh Cavalry sat their mounts, awaiting his order to dismount. He let them sit a moment before he gave it, his blue eyes in his sunburned, dust-streaked face inspecting the first lines critically. Some of the troopers looked all in, and those in back would be even worse, for the new recruits were always assigned to the rear. He hoped they had sense enough to take full advantage of a few hours' rest. This must be assumed to be a temporary bivouac. Tents were not to be set up, except for the one needed for headquarters. Only the necessities for the evening meal were to be removed from the packs. If the Crow scouts he had sent ahead located the Sioux, there would be a night's march ahead.

He gave the awaited order verbally, for there had been no bugles sounded since the regiment reached the valley of the Rosebud. The twelve companies—585 enlisted men and 31 officers—wheeled their mounts into the familiar lines for making camp. The interpreters and the other Indian scouts had not waited. They were already on foot, leading their ponies to the stream to drink.

It was a good campsite, the general told himself, one of the best he had yet found. It was too bad that in all likelihood they would not be staying. He always chose the campsites himself, riding ahead of the regiment with a few scouts, and he took pride in the knowledge that the men of the Seventh boasted of his skill in finding new trails and good campsites. He well knew they were quick to criticize other things about him, saying that he drove his men and animals too hard and changed his mind too often. But he got results. That was the important thing.

He removed his wide-brimmed hat, and as he hit it against the top of his high boot, dust flew and scattered. There was a small breeze, and it felt

strangely cool on his close-cropped head. Even after three months he wasn't used to the absence of the long blond hair that had once touched his shoulders. Sometimes he wondered about the whim that had caused him to cut it short. He had worn it long so many years, all through the Civil War and during earlier Indian campaigns, that it had become a trademark. Newspaper writers always mentioned it in their glowing accounts of his victories, and the Indians pointed it out in the name they called him, Long Hair. Well, his hair was anything but long now. It was shorter than any trooper's. Maybe the Sioux wouldn't even recognize him when he finally caught up with them.

He glanced impatiently toward the men who were putting up his tent. They worked with remarkable dispatch, but every minute's delay was an irritation. He knew he had pushed his troops hard for the last two days, but there was so little time. Only by pushing and driving had he managed to arrive a day ahead of Terry's reckoning.

General Terry was in charge of the expedition, including the Seventh Cavalry, that had been sent out to round up the Sioux and Cheyenne under Sitting Bull and force them onto reservations. They couldn't be allowed to roam free as they had always done. Settlers were coming in and needed the land. They complained that their stock was being run off, their cabins fired. Sometimes they were massacred, and of course the miners in the sacred hills of the Sioux were never safe. The savages had torn down telegraph lines and ripped out sections of the newly laid railroad tracks, a wanton destruction that could not be tolerated.

Washington had received a lot of complaints, and had tried to make treaties. Some of the tribes had signed and were now living snug and harmless on the reservations set up for them. But others of the Plains Indians, notably the Sioux and Cheyenne, refused to sign, and eventually the army had been called in. General Terry had been ordered to find these Indians and conduct them to the agencies, by force if necessary.

The difficulty had been to locate them. The Sioux were as elusive as the end of a rainbow. When you got where you were sure they were, they were no longer there.

A command under General Crook, which had been crossing the Rosebud Valley on its way to an assignment in the south, had actually encountered Sioux and engaged them in battle. The force of Indians had been so large that Crook had to retreat. But only a day or so later, Major Reno had led an exploratory expedition into the same valley and reported having seen nothing but old, deserted campsites.

Custer's lip curled as he thought of it. If that had been his command, instead of Reno's, he would have pushed on. Cold campsites led to fresh ones. Major Reno was new to Indian warfare. He needed a baptism under fire.

General Terry had been of the same opinion. He was convinced that the Sioux who had recently been in the Rosebud Valley had probably moved on to the valley of the Little Big Horn. He had divided his forces in order to intercept the Indians and pin them between two armies.

General Custer with twelve cavalry companies had been sent from the mouth of the Rosebud River up into the valley until he reached the deserted camps seen by Reno. He was then to follow the trails and, if possible, overtake the Sioux.

Gibbon's infantry, a smaller command but reinforced by three Gatling guns, was to march down the Big Horn Valley, in order to intercept the Sioux should they attempt to escape from Custer in that direction.

While General Terry had not set a date for rendezvous, he had roughly calculated the time. The two forces should come together on June 26, unless of course one of them was delayed to do battle with the Sioux. And that was exactly what Custer expected to do. He wanted to find the Sioux and bring them to their knees before the arrival of Gibbon's infantry.

That was the way the newspaper headlines would read: "Custer's Seventh Cavalry Subjugates Sitting Bull and the Sioux"! And to make sure that the papers got all the details, he had brought along Mark Kellogg of the New York *Tribune*.

Custer had a feeling that some of his officers suspected what he had in mind. Captain Benteen, for instance. Although scrupulously polite, the captain always regarded young Kellogg with that quizzical smile of his. But Benteen knew better than to say anything. Custer was his superior officer—younger, cleverer, and a hero in the eyes of the American public. No one but the War Department and his own family and troops had ever heard of Benteen. No one had ever written him up in the newspaper. Still he was a good soldier and an able officer. Custer was glad to have him along. The Seventh was short of experienced officers. It was even short of enlisted personnel. The usual cavalry company had sixty men, and the average in these twelve companies was considerably less than that.

He glanced over his shoulder impatiently. The men had almost finished with the tent. As soon as the scouts returned, he'd call an officers' meeting.

For the hundredth time since the Seventh Cavalry started off on their own, Custer thanked his lucky star that General Terry had elected to accompany Gibbon's infantry. Had he stayed with the cavalry, Terry would have received the glory when they defeated the Sioux.

For a moment he recalled one disastrous time that his lucky star deserted him. It had happened three months ago during the impeachment proceedings for Secretary of War Belknap. Custer had been called to Washington to testify. He hadn't wanted to go, but it was an order. When he arrived, he had told the truth about the Indian agents in the west. The agents had been withholding money and passing out weevily flour and spoiled meat to the Indians. It was unfortunate that the brother of the President of the United States was involved, but a gentleman had to tell the truth under oath.

President Grant had taken his revenge. He had snatched the promised command of the expedition against the Sioux out of Custer's hands and given it to Terry. If his luck hadn't given out that time, Custer would have been in complete charge.

But his lucky star was with him again. He was a day ahead of schedule. He had one day, perhaps even two, to discover Sitting Bull's camp and whip the Sioux into shape. Custer wanted to do it alone, with the Seventh Cavalry. He wanted to share the glory with no one.

The troopers assigned to the tent detail had finished their task, and Custer sent his adjutant, Lieutenant Cooke, to inform the officers of a conference after the meal. Supper would be very soon, for cooking fires were burning near the face of the cliff and the big coffeepots, hanging over them, were already beginning to give off steam. Horses, their muzzles dripping water, were being led up from the river, headed for their own suppers. It would have to be supplemented with oats from their rapidly depleting supply, Custer thought ruefully. The grass here was too short to provide enough nourishment for hard-working cavalry horses. Recently it had been nibbled close by another herd of hungry grazers, and there had not been time for it to grow back.

Sioux ponies, he thought as he entered his tent, Sioux ponies, probably now pastured just over the Wolf Mountains ahead and in the valley below!

Captain Frederick Benteen walked among his men, his eyes noting with approval the neatly placed saddles, the Springfield rifles in positions of readiness in case of emergency, the freshly filled canteens, the rubbed-down horses, each with its nose in an oat bag.

He had a genuine affection for his men, which was more than he had for most of the officers in the Seventh. His troopers were good men. They rode hard, worked hard, fought hard, and they had a proper respect for discipline. Not a one of them was like the troopers in the Wild I Company, led by Captain Keogh. The men of I Company were always looking for a chance to kick over the traces, sometimes with the approval of Keogh himself. Company H was a good company, and Benteen was proud of it. He wished the men might have the night's rest they so justly deserved. But at least they'd have a meal, if you could call bacon, hardtack soaked in water, and coffee a meal.

He paused to relight his pipe, and when it was going, he continued walking, a burly figure in dusty blues with a shock of white hair that rose on his head like a turban.

Captain Benteen was not a young man. He was the oldest officer in the Seventh, but there was no abler soldier in the regiment. He had proved that many times over during the Civil War, when he had been a colonel. Sometimes it rankled a little, to be reduced to the peacetime status of captain

and to be serving under a much younger man, but soldiering was all he knew. And in a way he was lucky to be here. There were more former officers looking for work than there were assignments to give out.

As the men picked up their tin cups and plates to start for the fires, Benteen was joined by Major Marcus Reno, the second-in-command, who asked if he'd heard whether the Crow scouts had returned.

Benteen hadn't. He pointed toward a fire set apart from the others where the Indian scouts were preparing their own meal. If Reno really

wanted to know, he could probably find out there
—or he could ask the general.

Major Reno declined both suggestions. He
avoided direct communication with the scouts
whenever possible, and he wouldn't ask the general
the time of day.

Benteen nodded. Dislike of General Custer was
the one thing he and Major Reno had in common.

The officers of the Seventh Cavalry were divided
into two factions—those who disliked their commanding officer, and those who admired and re-
vered him. Part of the dislike, Benteen admitted
honestly, was jealousy of someone who had risen
so fast in rank and whom the newspapers had
turned into an American idol. As for himself, he
had another reason, and he made no secret of it.

In a previous Indian campaign, several years
past, Custer had withdrawn without making certain that all his forces were intact. Later the bodies
of a small detachment that had been cut off
from retreat were found badly mutilated. Benteen,
who had been a friend of the officer in charge of
the group, would never forgive his commanding
officer. He was formally polite in Custer's presence
and obeyed every order without question, but there
was no friendship between them.

As they walked to their own meal, both Reno

and Benteen were silent. They knew how much depended on this campaign against the Sioux. The War Department was insistent, and the orders were clear. The Sioux and their allies must be delivered to assigned reservations, by force if necessary.

Major Reno thought yearningly of the regiment he had commanded with distinction during the War Between the States. What he wouldn't give to have them behind him right now. They had been trained soldiers—not riffraff, some of them foreigners who could hardly speak English! The new recruits who had arrived shortly before the expedition set out were poor horsemen and poorer shots. Reno had discovered that the few times he had tried to conduct target practice. As for the Indian scouts, they were the worst of all! Major Reno, whose previous dealings with Indians had been conducted behind the walls of the fort, didn't trust any of them. They might pretend to be friendly, but they were all savages underneath.

Captain Benteen was thinking about his commanding officer. He wondered exactly what Custer had up his sleeve this time. He glanced over his shoulder at the troopers lining up before the fires. Some of them looked ready to drop. A good night's rest was what they needed, not a forced march. It had been a long, hard day starting at five in the morning, and it was now after eight at night. They had covered thirty miles, and all those Indian signs along the way had made some of the recruits jumpy. Not only were the men tired, but the horses were all but played out, too. The Seventh was twenty-four hours ahead of schedule, and what everyone needed was some sleep. But that wasn't Custer's way. Custer was never tired, and he expected his men to be the same.

Benteen wondered, as they all did, how big Sitting Bull's camp would be. There had been much speculation about it, and everyone agreed it would be large. The Hunkpapa had been joined by some of the other Teton Sioux, notably Crazy Horse's Oglala, and possibly a few Cheyenne as well. Some of the young bucks from the agencies were reported missing, and they had probably flocked to Sitting Bull's command. Custer was inclined to set the figure at fifteen hundred Indians, although the scouts maintained the number would be much larger. Benteen himself couldn't even hazard a guess.

The scouts were discussing that very matter around their cooking fire now. By count the Indian scouts and their interpreters were equal to those of a regular cavalry company. Forty were Arikara, more commonly called Ree, blood enemies of the Sioux. Once they had been a large and powerful tribe, but disease had reduced their ranks by half. Because they lived in permanent villages, the better to grow corn and vegetables, they were no longer able to protect their former hunting preserves and had signed treaties with the government. But even the Sioux did not deny their courage, and when the offer came to serve as army scouts, many had been glad to sign on. The pay was good, sixteen dollars a month—three dollars more than a trooper received—with an additional twelve dollars for each pony furnished. But more important to them was the chance to atone for ancestral wrongs. Their hatred for the Sioux was undiminished, and they hoped to return with many scalps.

Because the country to be passed through was unfamiliar to the Ree, six Crow scouts from Gibbon's infantry command had been added. The Crow knew every ridge surrounding the Rosebud and Little Big Horn valleys, every stream and grassy stretch and trail. A few years before, all this land had belonged to them, but Sioux war parties had driven them away, claiming it for themselves.

It was not a new feud. The Crow and Sioux were

ancient enemies. Frequent raiding parties took place between the two tribes, ponies were stolen, scalps lifted, and coups counted. The Crow had been glad to join the white soldiers in their campaign against the Sioux, and the army was glad to have them. There were no better trackers, no fiercer warriers, than the Crow.

There were four interpreters, only one of whom was all white. Charley Reynolds—called Lonesome Charley by his own countrymen, and Lucky Man by the Indians because he seemed to lead a charmed life—was one of the most famous of the frontier scouts. He was a shy man who spoke only from necessity and kept much to himself.

Stocky Mitch Bouyer spoke English, Crow, and Sioux, and General Gibbon, to whose command he originally belonged, had told Custer that Bouyer was the only half blood he had ever known who could give distances in terms of miles. His most prized possession was a vest made of spotted pony fur, and he usually wore a headdress adorned with two stuffed woodpeckers and an eagle's feather.

Isaiah Dorman was a Negro, who had a knowledge of several tribal tongues. He had come up the Missouri in 1871, had married an Indian woman, and had known Sitting Bull and called him friend.

Later he had worked as a courier and mail carrier out of Fort Lincoln, but life at an army post had grown irksome. He wanted to return to the wild country, and had asked permission to accompany Terry's expedition.

One other interpreter had known Sitting Bull personally. Fred Girard had been taken prisoner by the Sioux and had lived with them for several years. Sitting Bull had adopted him, making him one of the tribe, but in time Girard had wanted to return to the life he had known before. He had run away, and now he was coming back as an interpreter for the Ree.

The three Crow, who had been sent ahead, reported back before the others finished their meal. There were signs of the Sioux, they said, many lodge trails. They all crossed the line of mountains dividing the two valleys and went down into the Little Big Horn. Some of the trails were fresh. All were wide.

Bloody Knife, one of the Ree scouts, asked if any of the newer trails was as large as the one they had found earlier when they crossed the Rosebud. That had been more than a mile wide, and so scratched by thousands of trailing lodge poles that the ground looked almost as though it had been plowed.

No, Half-Yellow-Face told him. These were

smaller trails, but they all led in the same direction —to the valley.

"All these trails prove what we have already heard." Bloody Knife spoke in sign language, so all could understand. "The young men of Red Cloud's Oglala and Spotted Tail's Brulé have left their reservations to join Sitting Bull and Crazy Horse. There will be other trails, too, of Miniconjou and Sans Arc and Cheyenne."

"The Sioux are confident of victory," Stabbed, one of the oldest and most experienced scouts, added in sign language. "They would not have left those messages if they had not wanted us to read them."

The firelight gleamed on the circle of brown faces, and black eyes grew solemn with remembrance.

Earlier that day they had passed a deserted campsite larger than any they had found before. Still standing was the framework of several old lodges. The largest must have been used for a Sun Dance, and in it hung the scalp of an unknown white man. There was evidence that much medicine had been made there recently, and there were other signs for Ree and Crow eyes to read.

Sand had been smoothed, and pictures drawn of pony soldiers, cavalry. Mitch Bouyer had tried

to tell the general that this was proof that the Sioux knew they were coming, but Long Hair would not open his ears.

In one of the empty sweat lodges there was a ridge of sand dividing pictures of dead soldiers and Indians. The soldiers' heads were pointed toward the Indians, which meant that the Sioux medicine was strong, and the soldiers would be defeated.

But that was not the worst.

Placed on an arrangement of stones were the skulls of a bull and a cow buffalo. A pole slanted toward the cow's skull, and the meaning was clear to Ree and Crow alike: When the Sioux were over-

taken, they would fight like a buffalo bull, and the pony soldiers would run from them like women.

Even then Long Hair would not open his ears. He only repeated something he had said many times before: "The Seventh Cavalry can take care of all the Indians on the North American continent."

When the interpreters told them, the Ree and Crow scouts could only shake their heads.

"It is as I told Long Hair." Bloody Knife stood up, so that those in the back could see his hands. "The gathering of the enemy is like the new grass in springtime. They are too many for us. But Long Hair will not believe me. He will lead us against them without waiting for Lame Hip [General Gibbon] and his foot soldiers to arrive. Sitting Bull and Crazy Horse are not men without sense. They have their scouts, and their eyes are upon us. They are waiting just over the ridge in the valley. We will have a big fight, a losing fight. As for myself, I know what will happen. My sacred helper has given me warning, and I will not see the setting of tomorrow's sun."

From the back of the circle, Lucky Man Charley Reynolds rose to his feet and stepped forward. In his hands he held the leather pouch, his "war bag," which he always carried on his saddle.

"I feel as does my brother, Bloody Knife," he told them. "Tomorrow will also be the end of me. Anybody who wants my stuff can have it right now."

As he began passing out tobacco, a sewing kit, shirts, and small articles, many of the scouts turned their heads away. They did not want the gifts. Those who accepted did so reluctantly. It was a bad sign for Lucky Man to be giving away his possessions.

The gloom persisted throughout the meal. Even those who had been ravenous had lost their appetites. Before they finished, they were joined by Lieutenant Varnum, who was in charge of the scouts. They called him Knife Face, and he had earned their respect since he never asked more of them than he was willing to do himself.

The march was to be resumed that night, he told them. The regiment would rest for two hours more, then go on. Some of the scouts, as usual, would lead. Bouyer and two of the Crow were to take the right of the trail. Bloody Knife and two other Ree would be responsible for the left. A third group would accompany Knife Face himself and stay in the middle. They would leave now, and the three parties would rendezvous at the Crow's Nest, a round knoll atop the dividing line of hills.

Without comment those designated arose and started for their ponies. After a long day it would be a trying night. They must move cautiously through the darkness, pausing often to listen to the howling of the wolves and the hoot of an owl, for those might be signals of an enemy scout. They must watch always for the small gleam of a fire, for some sick one who might have been left behind by those who proceeded on the trail. There might even be bad spirits, for such were known to roam the world after the sun had closed his great eye. But most important, they must search for signs of their common enemy—the Sioux.

JUNE 25, 1876

12:30 a.m.—2 p.m.

The night's march got off to a bad start. Custer's orders had been to move at eleven o'clock, but the packtrain mired down crossing a small stream, which someone immediately dubbed "Mud Creek." Heavy-eyed troopers dozed on their mounts for an hour and a half while the packers pushed and pulled and swore at their tired mules in an effort to get them across.

Custer waited impatiently, and when the last animal was out of the water, he led the way with Girard as his interpreter and Half-Yellow-Face and Bloody Knife as scouts.

The general was not tired, although he had had no more sleep than any of his men. That was the trouble, the troopers often complained to one another; Custer was never tired. He needed less sleep

than a bear in summer, and he expected everyone else to be the same.

As he rode through the darkness, he was filled with questions that Girard was kept busy translating. How many Indians did they think were in Sitting Bull's camp? Not less than twenty-five hundred, possibly three thousand, Girard told him patiently. He had answered this question many times, and so had the other scouts, but the general did not believe them and asked it again and again.

If that was so, they would probably be scattered in many small camps, decided Custer shrewdly, and he wanted to make sure to get them all. He didn't want a single Sioux to escape.

He need not worry about small camps, Bloody Knife assured him. When they located the main camp, the regiment would meet all the Indians they wanted.

Custer was not convinced. Perhaps instead of waiting through the day in the wooded ravine as the scouts advised, it would be better to continue on. Perhaps they should cross the mountains at daybreak and boldly enter the valley of the Little Big Horn. He was prepared to do battle, if necessary to the complete annihilation of the enemy, and they must be caught unaware.

No, his three companions declared quickly, a day's rest for the men and horses while the scouts searched out the Sioux was the best plan.

Behind the leaders the men of the Seventh Cavalry followed as best they could. There was no more dozing on horseback. The night was so black their eyes were useless. Instead they had to depend on other senses. When a man could not smell the dust kicked up by the horses before him or hear the rattle of the preceding trooper's tin cup against the horn of his saddle, he knew he was off the trail.

It was a relief to everyone when Custer finally called a halt. Most of the men sagged down in their saddles, with their reins in their arms, and slept.

The general reminded himself that under present conditions it would require two hours to reach the foot of the Wolf Mountains, the dividing line between the two valleys. It would take only half that long in daylight. A night march was always harder than one by day, and even he was beginning to feel the strain. It was just two o'clock.

Three hours later the camp was astir, with fires blazing to boil coffee and the horses being led down to a small creek to water. Both gestures were useless. The creek water contained so much alkali that the horses would not touch it, and boiling did nothing to improve its flavor. The coffee was thrown on the ground.

But the cooking fires served one purpose. The smoke guided two Ree scouts straight to the camp. Red Star and Bull had been sent by Knife Face Varnum from the Crow's Nest, the high knoll that overlooked the Little Big Horn Valley.

The general's eyes gleamed as he read the penciled words in the lieutenant's note.

At first dawn, before there were heat waves to cloud the view, the scouts in the Crow's Nest had seen the hostile camp, Custer told his officers. The intervening bluffs had obstructed sight of the whole area, but the visible flat was white with lodges, and the air was hazy with the smoke of cooking fires. On the benches above the Little Big Horn was a pony herd so large it covered the earth like a carpet.

Custer called for his horse. He was completely refreshed, and this was something he had to see for himself. The Sioux encampment at last! Sitting Bull and all his warriors totally unaware that Custer and the Seventh Cavalry were on their trail.

He set out immediately to join Varnum and the scouts, leaving orders that the regiment was to continue on to a wooded ravine at the base of the mountains. It was in this spot that the scouts advised that the Seventh Cavalry lie hidden through tomorrow, awaiting the day on which General Terry reckoned both forces would enter the valley.

Bull did not return with the general to the Crow's Nest. He was poorly mounted on a shaggy pony not much larger than a Newfoundland dog, and the animal was almost played out. When he reported to Girard, he made no effort to conceal his scorn.

"What is it?" asked Girard curiously. "Why is my brother's heart so filled with anger?"

The smoke of the fires, Bull told him contemptuously. From the Crow's Nest it was plainly visible, and it had led him and Red Star unerringly to the encampment. Did the white leaders think the Sioux were blind and used no scouts? Soon Sitting Bull would know the soldiers were here and would guess their plans. He would fight, and he had more Sioux than there were bullets in the belts of the soldiers.

Girard nodded soberly. He was sure that the Ree was right.

By eight-thirty the command was again on the march. This time everyone was in high spirits, and the troopers laughed and joked with one another. There was much chuckling over the plight of Sergeant Curtis who with two men from F Company had been sent back to retrieve a box of hardtack, which had been lost from one of the packs. They could be in for a long, dusty ride, since no one was sure where the box had broken loose.

By the time the troops reached the deep, well-wooded ravine where both men and horses could take cover, the sun was beginning to burn through their blue wool shirts. The swarms of flies, which had pestered them all the way on the Rosebud, grew even larger. They had never seen so many flies, the men agreed. They drove the poor horses crazy.

Not all the scouts had stayed with the line of march. As usual, groups had gone out on either side, and not long after the arrival at the ravine, they returned with the report that the Sioux were well aware of the presence of the enemy. Two small mounted parties had been sighted, observing the troops from a distance. When the Sioux realized they had been seen, they had ridden away in the direction of their camp. Moreover there were fresh pony tracks in a ravine close to this one where the men were to lie hidden.

Soon afterward, Sergeant Curtis and his men returned with the recovered box of hardtack. They had found a Sioux attempting to open it on the trail while two of his friends sat their horses nearby.

Sergeant Curtis had fired his pistol, but obviously he had missed. The Sioux had dropped the box, leaped on his pony, and the three Indians had galloped away out of range along the ridge.

"I knew well enough they had scouts ahead of us," said Charley Reynolds wryly. "But I didn't think they'd have others trailing along behind to pick up stuff dropped by our careless packers."

The troopers who overheard the remark laughed, but the other scouts nodded soberly. Charley hadn't been making a joke. No Indian war party would have advanced with such disorganized confusion.

General Custer returned from the Crow's Nest, and to everyone's surprise he ordered the bugler to sound "Officers' Call." For the past two days there had been only verbal commands. Now there was no more need for silence, he told them. Lieutenant Varnum had convinced him that the Sioux were well aware of the presence of the regiment, and any further attempts at concealment were useless.

Even with field glasses he himself had been unable to see anything in the valley of the Little Big Horn, but the scouts, whose vision was better than any white man's, and Lieutenant Varnum, whose eyes were almost as good, were quite definite. Before haze from the heat of the sun had risen to obscure the distance, they had seen a large Sioux encampment just ahead. Custer had decided to cross the mountains immediately, ride down into the valley, and attack. If they waited another day, it would give the Sioux time to scatter, and the tedious work of rounding them up would have to begin again.

His officers listened impassively. Custer was their commanding officer. He made the decisions and gave the commands. It was their duty to obey. But Mitch Bouyer was not so reticent. With two Crow scouts he had crept into the valley as close as he dared, and returning now, he interrupted the officers' conference to make his report.

"General, we saw that camp on the Little Big Horn. It's a big one—too big for you to tackle. Why, there are thousands and thousands of Sioux and a lot of Cheyenne down there."

"I shall attack them," declared Custer firmly. "If you are afraid, Bouyer—"

"I guess I can go wherever you do, General," the interpreter told him angrily. But he was determined to finish his report. Speaking in English and in sign language as well, for the benefit of the other scouts who now encircled the knot of officers, he described the Sioux camp in greater detail.

It was at least three miles long. There were hundreds and hundreds of lodges. Above and below were thousands and thousands of close-herded ponies. It was going to be a hard fight, a terrible fight.

Custer heard him through to the end, then calmly continued with his instructions. Every company commander was to select one noncommissioned officer and six privates and detail them to the packtrain, each man to lead two pack mules. Each commander was also to inspect his company and satisfy himself that men and horses were fit and ready for emergency. The troops would march in the order in which their commanders reported them ready.

First to report was Captain Benteen, and to H Company fell the honor of leading the advance. Last was Captain McDougall, and Company B was assigned the difficult task of guarding the slow moving packtrain.

The scouts were ordered ahead and told to steal or stampede the Sioux pony herd if they could. Ordinarily this would have been an assignment to gladden any Ree or Crow heart, for coups could be counted for stealing ponies, especially Sioux ponies. Today, however, they waited while Stabbed, one of the oldest and most experienced

among them, rubbed a bit of clay on each brown body in turn. It was special clay, and Stabbed had said many prayers over it until now it had become medicine to make a man brave and assure his safety in battle.

Not all the Ree believed in the efficacy of the medicine, however. Before he rode away, Bloody Knife looked up at the sun and in sign language told it, "I shall not see you go down behind the mountains tonight."

The Wolf Mountains, which separate the valleys of the Rosebud and the Little Big Horn, are not extensive, and the crossing was made in a short time. But the ground was rough, and the horses of the Seventh Cavalry had to climb up precipitous slopes that looked down into deep ravines and narrow gulleys, and later descend perilously on the other side.

The regiment reached the summit at high noon and was joined by Lieutenant Varnum and the scouts from the Crow's Nest. The valley of the Little Big Horn was not the level prairie they had imagined. It erupted in numerous knobby elevations, some of which spread out into ridges and short ranges of low hills. The river, fed by several small creeks, ran a tortuous course of curves and twists from east to west, and some of the twisting curves were so pronounced that for intervals the stream ran north and south.

Every eye squinted hopefully in the direction of Sitting Bull's supposed camp. They could see no lodges, no pony herds, for heat waves rose from the ground obscuring their view. But in the southwest, some fifteen or twenty miles away, the haze gathered in a light-blue cloud that the scouts claimed was smoke from the campfires of the Sioux. They headed in that direction.

Company H proudly led the advance. Captain Benteen deliberately set a fast pace, and the approving cheers of his men brought a twinkle to his eyes beneath their bristling brows. The blood bays of H Company were in good condition, and a short run wouldn't hurt them. It would stir up a little breeze, and the flies wouldn't have time to settle.

Almost immediately, however, the general caught up with them and curtly told the captain he was riding too fast. It was difficult for some of the others, particularly the packtrain, to keep up. Benteen immediately slowed his men to a walk, and shortly afterward came the call for the entire regiment to halt.

While the troopers perspired in the heat and the horses' tails flicked at flies, General Custer and his adjutant, Lieutenant Cooke, made the first division of troops since the regiment had marched into the Rosebud. These companies, H, D and K, commanded by Benteen, Captain Weir, and Lieutenant Godfrey, with a total of 125 men, were formed into one battalion under Benteen's command, and ordered to diverge to the south at an angle of 45 degrees.

The orders were given orally, and Benteen saluted and prepared to move out. As he passed Major Reno, he muttered that he was to go south and "pitch into anything I might come across."

He tried to tell himself it was sound strategy. If the Sioux attempted to escape, they would have to go north or south. On the north they would encounter Gibbon's infantry. His own men were expected to drive them back if they went south. Just the same, the order rankled. Unlike his commanding officer, Benteen had decided that the Seventh Cavalry was on the trail of several thousand Sioux, and he did not think it was necessary to scare up stragglers. He wondered if he was being sent on a senseless errand, one that would keep him out of the big battle. But he was a soldier. He obeyed the command, and the new battalion left at once.

Even before they were out of sight, Custer sent two additional orders after them, which did little to soothe the captain's feelings. Trooper Henry Voss carried instructions for Benteen to go on to the second line of bluffs if he found nothing upon reaching the first. The second messenger ordered him to go into the next valley if he found no Indians on the second bluffs.

Meanwhile the division of troops continued. Companies A, G, and M were formed into a second battalion under the command of Major Reno while Custer himself retained command of the other five: Captain Keogh's I Company, Captain Yates's F, Lieutenant Smith's E, Lieutenant Calhoun's L, with the general's brother, Captain Tom Custer, in command of Company C. The slow-moving packtrain under Captain McDougall's Company B—a total of 130 men—was to follow as best they could.

In columns of four, the commands of Custer and Reno followed a small creek that flowed from the divide toward the blue cloud in the southwest. The valley had widened, and the hooves of the horses and mules sent up an enormous screen of dust that hung on the hot, dry air and was plainly visible for many miles.

Before long the scent of smoke mingled with that of dust. They had come upon a burning tepee. Obviously since it was Sioux and belonged to their enemy, the Crow and Ree scouts had set it afire; and the dry lodge poles were now blazing furiously under the hot sun.

"It's a burial tepee," explained Lieutenant Varnum, who had ridden ahead with the scouts. "There's a dead warrior in it."

General Custer gave the order to halt. He had small interest in burial tepees or dead warriors, but his eyes examined curiously the surrounding terrain. Once a Sioux encampment had been made here. There were evidences of numerous lodge poles, the ashes of old cooking fires, and many of the bushes near the creek were broken and dis-

figured from being bent over to form wickiups.

The interpreter Girard had climbed a small hill just behind the old encampment. He turned, pointing with one hand into the valley below and cupping his mouth with the other to make his words carry straight ahead.

"There go your Injuns, General! Running like the devil."

With an exclamation Custer spurred his horse to reach the interpreter's side.

Some three miles away, on the opposite bank of the Little Big Horn River, he could see a small party of mounted warriors covering the withdrawal of a group of women and children with the pack animals and paraphernalia of a village.

It was exactly what Custer had been afraid of all the time! Sitting Bull's scouts had warned him of the approaching soldiers. The Sioux were breaking up their encampment. This group was riding toward, not away from, the spot where Varnum had reported the large encampment to be, but Custer could explain that easily enough. There must be several villages, all in flight.

He hurried back to the blazing tepee and ordered the scouts to pursue the Indians. They refused to go.

"If any man of you is not brave enough, I will

take away his weapons and make a woman of him," threatened Custer angrily.

"Tell him if he does the same to all his white soldiers who are not as brave as we are, it will take him a long time," taunted one of the Ree when Girard had translated the general's words.

This was considered a great joke by all the scouts, who laughed loudly as they continued to admire the blazing tepee.

A scout could not be forced to obey an order against his will, but the general knew someone who could. Major Reno with his three companies was just riding up.

Custer told his adjutant to give Reno the order to cross the river and attack the Indians. Custer himself would support the attack with the rest of the command. Then he added, "Tell him to take the scouts with him."

Major Reno accepted the order without question. His troops did not dismount, but started for the crossing of the Little Big Horn River some fifteen minutes away. The Ree scouts, perhaps shamed by the general's charge of cowardice, mounted their ponies and rode after the soldiers. In addition, Girard, Dorman, and Reynolds joined the party. Bouyer and the Crow were absent, having been sent ahead to scout, but Lieutenant Cooke and Captain Keogh rode to the river with Reno before returning to their own commands.

Previously the scouts had told the general that there were two crossings on the Little Big Horn River some five or six miles apart. The second was still ahead. It was approached by a ravine that the Indians called Medicine Tail Coulee. The first crossing was only a short ride from where they now were. A ridge of hills, some low but a few of significant height, ran parallel to the river, concealing it from the view of those on the trail.

Reno led his command at a brisk canter. On his arrival he found that the ford was from twenty-five to thirty feet wide and fairly deep. It took some time to cross, for the horses had gone without water since the night before and the troopers let them pause to drink. The major did not try to hurry them. A good cavalryman thinks first of his mount. By this time the Indian party was out of sight, but he knew the direction they had taken. A cavalry outfit should have no trouble overtaking a few savages.

They made the crossing in columns of twos: the mixed colors of Lieutenant Tom French's M troop first, then the coal blacks of Lieutenant Moylan's A, and finally the sorrels of Lieutenant McIntosh's G Company.

It was during this crossing that one of the scouts told Girard that the Sioux were not running away. They would likely come upriver to meet them. The interpreter reported this to Reno, but when he saw the major did not believe him, he himself re-crossed the river and gave the information to Lieutenant Cooke, who was just preparing to return to Custer. Lieutenant Cooke thought Girard's information was important, and promised to carry the news to the general.

Once across, Reno halted briefly to close up his command. His critical eye passed up and down the line. The men were a far cry from the spruce, well turned-out troops who had left Fort Lincoln on May seventeenth, a little more than a month ago. They were dirty, unshaven, and probably a little hungry. But their eyes were bright with anticipation, and their horses showed the meticulous care that only a cavalryman could give.

From the ring socket on each saddle hung a single-shot Springfield carbine, accurate and deadly up to six hundred yards. It was a fine rifle except when it was fired too rapidly. For then the breech became foul and the greasy cartridge jammed and had to be pried loose. Should that happen, each trooper carried the latest model six-shot single-action Colt army pistol at his hip. There were

nearly a hundred rounds of ammunition in each
web belt and saddle pocket, so he was well able
to take care of himself.

Major Reno had 134 officers and men, besides
the scouts, under his command, and he was well
pleased. At the last minute he had been joined by
Lieutenant Varnum and the small party of Ree
who had been scouting ahead. At the time Reno
had been a little horrified, for Varnum had swung
his hat about his head and shouted, "Thirty days'

furlough to the first man who gets a scalp!" But on reflection the major was relieved to have this addition to his command. The young officer had a way with Indians. Reno was glad he would not have to deal with the scouts himself.

As the command advanced over ground freshly cut by horses' hooves, he had a few misgivings. The grass had been cropped short by Indian ponies. Perhaps he should have paid more attention to the interpreter's warning at the ford, or at least have relayed the information. But it was not too late. He sent Trooper McIlhargy back to Custer with the reassuring message that he "had the enemy in front and that he was very strong."

This was hard country to travel, loose and sandy, studded with clumps of wild sage. On their left was the Little Big Horn River, hidden from view by tall cottonwoods and dense brush, and on the right were benchlands with a line of low hills just above.

As they rounded a curve, the valley widened, and they could see a great shifting cloud of dust ahead. It seemed to hover near the ground, moving and swirling, parting occasionally to give a glimpse within. Each time that happened, they could see Indians; how many it was impossible to determine. The whoops and yells came floating out of the cloud of dust as the Indians rode their ponies back and forth over a small area. Major Reno could not imagine what they were doing.

The battalion did not break its gallop, and some of the troopers began to cheer in answer to the war whoops. The major soon put a stop to that. They would have all the excitement they wanted later on, he told them. They'd better save their breath.

He was a little disconcerted when he saw the scouts leave to ride off at an angle from the troops, and he shouted angrily after them.

Lieutenant Varnum was at his side in an instant. It was all right, Knife Face Varnum assured him. Scouts were not expected to fight in line. Their duty was to run off the pony herd of the enemy. They had gone to see what they could do.

The major was embarrassed. Although he had earned a reputation as a brave and competent officer in the Civil War, this was his first Indian fight. Someone should have told him about the scouts before this, and not let him sound off like an idiot. He galloped on, leading his troops.

The dust made it hard to see, but there seemed to be white looming shapes ahead. The Sioux were still there. They had not yet pulled down their camp.

The troopers spurred their horses, and the dust cloud spread, widening on either side as the Indian riders were forced to give way. There were only a few of them after all. When the lodges loomed large before them, Major Reno gave the command to fire.

1:30 p.m.—4:00 p.m.

▲▲▲▲▲▲▲▲▲▲▲▲▲▲▲▲▲▲▲▲▲▲▲▲▲▲▲▲▲▲▲▲▲▲▲▲
▼▼▼▼▼▼▼▼▼▼▼▼▼▼▼▼▼▼▼▼▼▼▼▼▼▼▼▼▼▼▼▼▼▼▼▼▼

Gall, sometimes known as Walks-in-Red-Clothing, was uneasy. Earlier when the sun had been directly overhead, there had been mirror flashings by the scouts, which meant that the pony soldiers had crossed over the Little Chetish, called by the whites the Wolf Mountains, and were headed down into the valley of the Greasy Grass. Later the women returning from the hills, where they had been digging wild turnips, had reported the dust cloud of many horses. And still Sitting Bull continued to hold council with the Big Bellies, those wise and respected old men who had already made their coups and fought their battles, and were now content to sit in judgment on the younger warriors.

Gall was war chief of the Hunkpapa. He was a brave and fearless fighter. If it had been left to him, he would have marshaled his men and advanced to meet the pony soldiers. To this suggestion Sitting Bull closed his ears. His vision had shown him soldiers falling into camp. *Wakan Tanka* had his own plan. The Sioux must wait for the soldiers to come to them. All but Gall were content to abide by the first chief's decision.

Gall would never question the wisdom of *Wakan Tanka,* but he was glad to see that his young men were whetting and greasing their knives and lance heads, cleaning their guns and reloading the empty cartridges retrieved after the battle with Gray Fox on the Rosebud. That battle, in which the white soldiers had fled from the Sioux, had used up their supply of ammunition, but later a party had returned to the field and filled several unborn buffalo calf sacks with the good things left behind by the whites.

It was the custom of the wasteful soldiers to take from their belts a handful of shells at a time, which they then put down and later forgot as they moved off, fighting. Often the cartridges would jam if the guns were fired in too rapid succession, and they had to be pried loose with a knife. In battle a soldier might not take the time to do that, but would resort to the small gun in his belt. The Sioux had plenty of time and endless patience, and many of their firearms had been obtained in this way. Sitting Bull, as first chief, owned an 1873 model carbine Winchester, and there were a few more repeating rifles like it in the camp, but the majority of guns were old flintlocks and the Springfields retrieved from fallen soldiers. There were other valuables to be scavenged from a battlefield, too: lead from bullets flattened against rocks, arrow points, and iron shoes from dead cavalry horses. The Sioux wasted nothing.

Gall turned his gaze around the huge circle of Hunkpapa lodges, one for each family, although sometimes brothers and their wives and children shared a lodge in common. Before the entrances piles of sweet-scented herbage lay drying in the sun, for this was the Moon for Making Fat when grasses were gathered and the ponies grew plump after the long winter. Life was continuing just as though it were any other day, he thought resentfully. The young men cleaned their guns; the old ones dozed in the shade; the children played; and the women carried out those endless chores that women must do. It would be the same in every tribal circle, in the Blackfeet camp next to the Hunkpapa, the Sans Arc and Minicounjou circles beyond that, the Oglala and Brulé, and in the Cheyenne circle at the farthest end. Was he the only one uneasy? They knew the pony soldiers

were in the valley. Why did not Sitting Bull order them to prepare for war?

He walked restlessly away from the lodges to the bank of the Greasy Grass which flowed in front of the camp. Some fifteen miles to the north these waters joined with those of the Big Horn River, and because the melting snows were late, the stream ran high, swift, turbulent, and cold. The channel made too many bends for him to see either of the crossings: the one downstream in front of the Cheyenne camp, which led up into Medicine

Tail Coulee on the northern bank, or the first crossing upstream above the Hunkpapa lodges. Both were natural fords, made by *Wakan Tanka* for man and beast.

The sprawling encampments were on the south bank several feet above the river, and the land behind the lodges rose gradually into a great expanse of grassy meadow where the pony herd was tethered. Gall had never seen so great a herd at one time, and he doubted if anyone else had. The hungry, always-nibbling mouths of some twenty-five thousand ponies made short work of any meadow, and it was good that they planned to move at the next sun.

But now, today, providing the holy man of the Cheyenne was right, there would be fresh meat for the wolves before the sun closed its great eye. The ponies should not be grazing the last blades from the meadow. They should be brought down to the lodges. Their tails should be tied up, as was the custom for war, and proper paint should be applied to their flanks. They should be prepared for battle, and the young warriors should also prepare themselves.

Across on the northern bank of the river were ash-gray bluffs, their crests just visible above the green brush that crowded the bank. Gall stared hard at the bluffs, wondering about the white soldiers who were said to be riding toward them. From here he could see nothing, and he turned back to the lodges.

The Big Bellies were still sitting in the shade cast by their yellow-painted council lodge. They wore decorated shirts, with quilled bands running down the arms and quilled neckpieces in squares or medallions at their throats. They stirred the warm air and brushed away flies with fans made of buffalo tail mounted on short sticks.

In his younger days each had been a chieftain or, at least, a holy man. Only Sitting Bull still served in office. The others had retired, giving way to those who were younger and more vigorous. But because they had gleaned many honors and amassed much wisdom with their years, they were greatly honored.

Although Sitting Bull was of the highest rank, he was hardly distinguishable from the other old men today. He sat and fanned flies, a single feather in his braided hair, and his broad, square face painted red, since that was the color most pleasing to the sun, was wreathed in smiles. To look at him now, Gall found it hard to believe that Sitting Bull knew that the white soldiers were riding this way. But he did know. He had known since the sun was overhead, and now it had traveled more than the distance of a lodge pole in the sky.

A new party of Indians rode into camp. There were twenty or thirty warriors and a group of women and children with their pack animals and loaded travois. Gall hardly gave them a second glance. Every day saw newcomers join one of the seven circles. In the beginning it had been exciting to watch the camp swell and grow in size, but it had happened so often that he had come to take it for granted. These newcomers were not Hunkpapa. Someone had directed them on to one of the other circles.

Then he saw two men he did know, Fat Bear and Brown Buck, two of the young braves who had been sent across the river to round up stray horses. They rode in on lathered ponies and headed straight for the lodge that sheltered the Big Bellies. Gall walked closer that he might overhear the report to Sitting Bull.

They had been on the other side of the Chetish Mountains, said Fat Bear. In their search for horses they had crossed a soldiers' trail early that morning. On the trail they had found a lost box filled with hard bread, the kind the soldiers ate. Deeds had dismounted and was about to break it open when some of the soldiers returned. They fired their small guns, and a bullet hit Deeds in the back. He managed to get on his horse and ride away with the others, but he had died of the wound before they reached camp.

Gall did not wait to hear Sitting Bull's reply. He started away from the protected lodge of the Big Bellies toward the far edge of the Hunkpapa camp, the side near the first river crossing. As he walked, he saw dust rising in a streamer above the conical tops of the lodge poles, and he knew that the moment of Sitting Bull's vision was at hand. The soldiers were preparing to fall into camp.

"Hi-ya," he shouted. "Every warrior to his horse. The soldiers come!"

In an instant all was confusion. Old men began shouting advice. Young ones dashed for their horses and arms. Women grabbed their babies and ran as fast as their moccasined feet would take them. Children became lost from their mothers and cried. Dogs barked, and because no one stopped them, they continued barking. The few favorite ponies, tethered close to their owners' lodges, pawed at the ground and whinnied nervously.

A half-dozen boys, too young as yet to serve as warriors, had been playing in the sun. Gall turned to them, for there was no one else. They were to mount the nearby ponies and ride back and forth, stirring up a dust screen. It might confuse the soldiers and give the warriors more time to reach their mounts.

Proud and excited, the boys did as they were told. Their young voices shouted the old war cry of their people, and for a moment there came an answer from the blue-coated soldiers riding iron-shod horses toward them. Then the voices stopped.

The dust swirled and eddied as the unarmed

boys rode back and forth, but finally they had to fall back. The soldiers were upon them. Rifles cracked and bullets flew. There were screams from the women who had not yet found their children, and one of the lodges burst into flame.

The village was not long undefended. As fast as the Sioux were mounted, they rode out to meet the enemy. There was no time for saddles, no time to paint for battle, and every moment their vengeful number grew larger. They used their horses as screens, grasping the mane and sliding down one side to aim over the animal's back. They fired their ancient flintlocks and the more trustworthy bows of ashwood with iron-tipped arrows.

All but Gall. His had been the blazing tepee, and one of his wives and two children lay dead within. It had taken only a second in passing to make that clear to him, and seeing, his heart grew large with hate. He threw away all weapons but his hatchet, for only hand-to-hand combat could avenge this wrong.

Without thought to his own safety, Gall rode to one white soldier after another, pulling them from their horses and wielding his deadly weapon. For a moment he forgot that he was war chief. His one thought was to kill.

The white soldiers dismounted, and some of

their number led their horses back into a grove of trees. They formed a long line, each man firing from his knees, but the Sioux were not daunted. They poured into the field, yelling, firing, circling, each man secure in *Wakan Tanka*'s promise of victory.

Crazy Horse rode among them shouting advice, and because he had powerful medicine, the Sioux gave ear to his words. They tried to encircle the single line, hoping to close the enemy in a trap, but the soldiers fell back, firing as they went, and would not be drawn in.

Although dust and smoke hung so heavily in the air it was almost impossible to see, some of the Sioux, experts in the art of horse stealing, had been prepared for and had turned back a small party of Ree scouts attempting to creep through on the side. The Ree returned to the soldiers who by now had broken their long foot line and started for their mounts. They retreated, firing, into the grove of trees.

The lodges of the Hunkpapa and the Blackfeet Sioux were closest to the crossing used by the soldiers, and as the first to be attacked, they made up most of the initial fighters. They laughed to see the soldiers hurrying toward the trees. Everything was going as Crazy Horse had said.

"Be strong!" His voice had been loud during the battle, and he had shouted the words again and again. "Make them shoot three times fast, so their guns will fail. Then you can knock them down with your clubs."

Many had taken his advice, and gun after gun

had jammed and been discarded. Now the ground was littered with dead and wounded soldiers and their firearms, while only two Sioux warriors, Dog-with-Horns and Chased-by-Owls, had fallen to the bullets of the whites.

Seeing the retreating soldiers, the Hunkpapa and Blackfeet with shouts of triumph fell upon the rifles of the dead and wounded. They did not stop now to extract the jammed cartridges. That could come later.

Gall had recovered slightly from his initial rage, and now he gave the call of leadership. Some of his braves followed to surround the timber where the pony soldiers had taken shelter. There, leaving their horses, they began to creep through the trees, moccasined feet silent on the dry ground, war clubs and hatchets raised to readiness.

Their presence was discovered, however, and the soldiers began to ride out of the woods. By ones and twos they came, and then in a great rush with the quickly remounted Sioux after them. Whooping, firing arrows, each Indian slapped another's pony with his whip, so there was no chance of turning back. On they came, racing hard after the galloping hooves of the big cavalry horses.

Gall saw one of the Ree scouts ride close to the big horse which carried the officer in charge.

At that moment one of the Sioux fired his flintlock, and the bullet hit the scout full in the head. Gall laughed aloud when he saw the terror on the white officer's face as the scout's blood spattered his blue coat. The war chief pounded hard on his pony's sides, but it was no use. The army horse was frightened. With a spurt of frenzy he carried his rider far ahead.

The whites were headed for the river, riding at a fast gallop. They had formed themselves into a rough V, with the point leading, and the Sioux pressed closely on either side. It was difficult to see, for the dust followed like streaming banners, but Gall knew that they were headed for the upper crossing. He shouted a cry, and a party of Sioux moved out, following his lead, to close the way. The pony soldiers had to continue on down the bluff.

Farther along, the leader must have decided to make a try at fording the river where there was no crossing, for when Gall caught up the second time, they were jumping their horses into the river. The opposite bank was eight feet high, abrupt and slippery, but fear was strong and urged them on.

The Sioux stood on the bank, shooting arrows and laughing as they watched the mad scramble in the water. Some of them urged their own ponies across, and a few rode to their death, because not all the soldiers were panicked. One of them turned in his saddle and shot a young warrior through the heart, then took his scalp. Another delayed to gather up a loose Indian pony, then took a few shots at the pursuing warriors.

Gall stayed only long enough to see that the whites were urging their big horses up one of the bluffs. He knew that they would attempt to make a stand on the crest, and that there were plenty of young, hot-blooded braves to hold them there.

He himself, with most of the Hunkpapa warriors, turned back. A messenger had arrived with news of a long dust cloud rolling from the west along the bluffs. More pony soldiers were making for the second crossing opposite the Cheyenne camp.

2:00 p.m.–3:30 p.m.

For a hundred yards or so, Custer's battalion followed Major Reno's force toward the crossing. Then without warning the general changed his mind. He gave the signal to turn and continue on along the bluffs in the direction they had previously been taking.

Bugler John Martin, born Giovanni Martini, was riding close behind the general's big sorrel, Vic, and he was hard put to check his white horse and follow. His was a stupid horse, he told himself resentfully, not even a proper cavalry mount.

The white horses had been commandeered from the bandsmen at the time Custer's and Gibbon's forces separated. The bandsmen had joined Gibbon's infantry, and their horses had been given to the Seventh Cavalry as replacements. They were being used by the buglers because white was easier to see on the field. John Martin had been assigned one this morning when his own captain, Benteen, had told him to report to Custer as orderly bugler for the day.

Martin was not overly pleased with the assignment. He would have preferred to stay with his own company. He had not been too long in America, and his English still left something to be desired. He was used to the men in Company H, and they to him. He knew that they sometimes made little jokes about him, calling him "Dago" and "Wop," but Trooper Windolph who had come from Germany only a few years before said that would pass. At first they had called Windolph "Dutchy" and "Sauerkraut," but now he had become "Charley." Someday Martin would be called only John.

For a mile or so the general led his troops at a gallop, which made the guidons snap in the hot, dry air. There were two of them, and they went wherever Custer did. One was a red and blue swallow-tailed pennant, emblazoned with white crossed sabers and a large gold seven. The other was a fringed regimental standard with a gold eagle on a crimson field and the words Seventh U.S. Cavalry. They were carried by two color bearers riding directly behind the bugler.

From time to time the general left his command to gallop to the top of the line of bluffs that rose above the trail. He always returned shortly, Vic's hooves sending a shower of pebbles and dry earth rolling down the slope. Bugler Martin was in considerable awe of the commanding officer of the Seventh, and he kept his eyes straight ahead, never glancing to one side. When the big sorrel had again taken the lead and he once more faced the general's straight back and the rear of his wide-brimmed hat, Martin always breathed a little easier.

At length Custer raised his hand, signaling the bugler to sound halt. The five companies brought their lathered horses to a standstill at the base of a knoll rising from the line of bluffs. To Martin's surprise he was ordered to accompany the general to the top.

The white horse was streaming rivulets of sweat and was obviously growing tired. As he followed the general, Bugler Martin thought yearningly of his own blood bay off somewhere behind the ridges to the south. He wondered again where Company H had gone, but when he reached the summit of the hill, he forgot all about that.

Across the river, in the valley below, was an Indian encampment. Lodges gleamed white in the sunlight, circle after circle of them. Why, there were hundreds of them, peeping around the edge of a bluff. He could see women moving around the settlement, and children, dogs, and a few ponies, but there were no bucks, no warriors.

Martin remembered that Lieutenant Varnum had spoken with the general before riding off to join Major Reno's command. Perhaps he had told Custer of this encampment, and that was why the general had continued on, instead of following the others across the river.

Custer was laughing now. He said the Indian braves must all be sleeping in their tepees. Then he put field glasses to his eyes, scanning the other end of the valley. Martin wondered if he was looking for Major Reno's troops, but if he saw them, Custer made no comment. Instead he turned to wave his hat at the troopers waiting at the foot of the hill.

"Hurrah, boys, we've got them!" he shouted. "We'll finish them up and then go back to our station."

The troopers cheered as the general and his bugler rode back down the slope.

While Custer paused to speak with his adjutant, telling him what he had seen, Mitch Bouyer held a brief conference with his scouts. At the conclusion all the scouts but Stabbed, the only Ree who had refused to accompany Reno, turned their horses and rode away.

Custer angrily demanded an explanation.

He had sent the Crow away, the interpreter told him calmly. They had finished their job of leading the soldiers to the encampment. Scouts were not required to fight unless they wanted to. Fighting was for soldiers. However, since the general seemed to doubt Bouyer's courage, the interpreter himself would ride down into the valley. Stabbed also wished to go. They would match their courage against Long Hair's any day.

The general said no more. He gave the order, and the battalion rode on at a fast gallop. They halted the second time near a deep ravine that led down in the direction of the river. Here he spoke to his bugler.

"Orderly, I want you to take a message to Captain Benteen. Ride as fast as you can and tell him to hurry. Tell him it's a big settlement, and I want him to be quick and bring the ammunition packs."

He spoke very fast, and Martin strained his ears to follow the hard English words.

Then Lieutenant Cooke spoke up. "Wait, Orderly. I'll give you a message."

He scribbled rapidly in a little book, tore out the leaf, and handed it to Martin. "Ride as fast as you can to Captain Benteen. Take the same trail we came down. If you have time and there is no danger, come back. But otherwise stay with your company."

"Yes, sir," said Martin. He briefly wondered about the stamina of his tired band horse, but that was nothing to trouble the general about. He turned his mount and started back.

He knew that he was the second messenger dispatched by Custer to the rear. At first sight of the village Sergeant Kanipe of Tom Custer's C Company had been sent back to hurry along Captain McDougall and the packtrain.

Once Bugler Martin looked over his shoulder. General Custer's five companies, 225 men, with Mitch Bouyer, Stabbed, the Ree, and Mark Kellogg, the newspaper reporter from the east, were riding toward the ravine that Bouyer called Medicine Tail Coulee. They were advancing at a gallop, with Lieutenant Smith's gray horse company in the middle.

2:00 p.m.—5:00 p.m.

When the sun had traveled the length of a lodge pole in its descent down the western sky, Chief Two Moon took his favorite pony to the river. He owned many ponies, and there were always young Cheyenne willing to help with their tending, but Two Moon cared for this one himself. The pony was a stallion, not large, and black as a mountain lake on a night without stars. He moved with the lightness of a bird, and he had the sense of a man in that he could understand every word that Two Moon spoke.

While the stallion dipped his muzzle in the stream and drank deeply, Two Moon bathed himself in the cold water, splashing it high on the chest marked with the lasting scars of the Sun Dance. Then he cupped his two hands and splashed the flanks and sides of his pony, and the stallion turned his head, seemingly to express his pleasure.

The watering of the ponies at the crossing at Medicine Tail Coulee had been going on all day, with men and animals coming and going and always others to take their place. The Cheyenne, Oglala, and Miniconjou brought their ponies here. The Brulé and Sans Arc used the little creek that separated their camp from that of the Blackfeet Sioux. Sometimes the Blackfeet used the creek, too, but more often they and the Hunkpapa found the first crossing farther up the Greasy Grass more convenient to their circles.

As he stood, letting the swift water swirl about his thighs, Two Moon saw many he knew who were here on similar errands: Hump of the Miniconjou and his brother, Iron Thunder; Low Dog, chief of the Oglala, besides many of his own Cheyenne tribesmen. They called to each other in friendship, speaking of last night's dances and of their journey toward the mountains after the next sleep. Then one of them cried out and pointed upstream. All eyes turned in that direction.

"Ai!" they exclaimed.

A great whirling of dust was rising above the lodges of the Hunkpapa. On the benchland above, there was movement like an army of creeping ants advancing on the grazing ponies. Then came the distant sound of gunfire.

The warriors lost no time. Each man leaped upon his pony's back. Brown heels pounded dripping flanks as each headed for his own tribal circle.

Among the Cheyenne lodges, all was confusion. Some of the women were already heading for the pony herds, while others were dismantling the lodges. Some of the young men had been sleeping, but now they were awake, each running for his weapons and his paint pots.

Two Moon rode into camp, shouting: "Woo woo! Ah-ay, ah-ay! Warriors to your saddles! White soldiers come!" To the women tearing down the lodge poles, he called, "Do not run away. Stay here and fight. I am Two Moon, your chief. I shall stay, even if I am to be killed."

The women left off at once. Cheyenne women, like their braves, were fearless fighters. Often they accompanied their men into battle, and always they were ready to perform necessary tasks, such as herding the captured ponies of the enemy or bringing in the wounded.

Two Moon went into his own lodge. Hastily he smeared the red and yellow paint of war on his face and secured his weapons: his feathered lance, his bow and arrow, and his rifle. At his belt was his knife, whetted to a thin edge.

When he came out, there was a rider from Crazy Horse, telling the Cheyenne that white soldiers had charged the Hunkpapa camp intent on killing the women and children. All the warriors were to come.

One of his wives had already saddled the black stallion, tied up the tail with buckskin, and hung the rope of braided rawhide from the saddle. Two Moon fastened one end of the rope to his belt with a slipknot. If he dismounted in battle, it would reduce the danger of losing his pony.

He leaped to the saddle, giving the ancient yell of the Cheyenne, "Hi-yi-yi!" It was the command for all warriors to watch the actions of their leader and do as he did.

On their way to the Hunkpapa camp they met many women hurrying away from the scene of battle. And when they reached the last circle, they could see that a few of the lodges were burning but that the white soldiers had been driven back.

There were dead soldiers on the flat beyond the camp, and someone said that the others were now hidden in the trees. Suddenly out they came, mounted, to gallop toward the river. After them came the Sioux, yelling and shouting, stirring up dust like a thick yellow blanket.

"Hi-yi-yi!" shouted Two Moon and the chieftains Little Horse and White Bull, and the Cheyenne followed after them as fast as they could gallop their small ponies.

The horses of the whites maintained their lead, for they were bigger and stronger. To keep up, the Indian ponies had to gallop hard, but they were more fleet of foot. They could dart in and out, like hummingbirds that flit from one flower to another, but their unshod feet tired more quickly than those of horses wearing shoes of iron.

Gall's Sioux cut off the trail to the first ford, but the white soldiers made a crossing farther up. On the opposite bank they headed for a hill, bleak and without cover, and there they were allowed to remain, guarded finally by a handful of boys and women. Iron Cedar had brought word that a second army of soldiers was approaching the second crossing at Medicine Tail Coulee. Their flags had come up over the northern ridges, and in the low places there had been glimpses of men's hats bobbing like fallen catkins on the surface of a swift river.

The Cheyenne led the way, but the Sioux were close behind: Crazy Horse and his Oglala, Gall and his Hunkpapa, the Minconjou under Fast Bear, Scabby Head with his Blackfeet, and the Sans Arc and the Brulé. They galloped their wiry ponies as fast as they could go, but they had no

fear that they would be too late. The trail beyond the bluffs used by the white soldiers was longer than the route through the tribal circles.

When they arrived, the flags were just visible above the crest at the crossing. Behind them came the white soldiers, riding slowly, cautiously, their big horses stumbling a little as they descended. A sure-footed Indian pony would not stumble so unless he was very tired. The whites had seen the massed Sioux and Cheyenne by this time, but they

did not falter. They rode on, a few hundred to meet the thousands.

Crazy Horse gave orders. He told the Cheyenne chiefs to lead their warriors up the left. With his Oglala and the Miniconjou, he advanced on the right. Gall, still bad-hearted from his loss, had

charge of all downstream to make sure that none
escaped. This much only could a war chief do—
assign to a tribe a certain area. After that, each
hot-blooded warrior fought his own battle separate
from the others, nor did he see the whole but only
his own efforts and accomplishments.

They crossed the river—the Cheyenne and all
the Sioux—to meet the white soldiers on the northern bank, each warrior confident of the outcome.
These were the white soldiers sent by *Wakan
Tanka*. They were falling into camp like grasshoppers, and soon all their hats would tumble off.

Midway down the slope, the bugle of the white
soldiers sang the order to dismount. Some knelt
while others stood erect, and their guns spoke fast
and loud. The blue smoke from the powder filled
the air above the Greasy Grass, and even the earth
seemed to shudder at the sound. It hid the sough-
ing of the wind which never ceased upon this slope.

Each Sioux and Cheyenne slipped low behind
his pony, protecting himself from the killing fire.
Some dropped into ravines to wait for the time
when it would cease. This was a fine place for an
Indian to do battle. The land was rough. There
were many coulees, and the trees and bushes along
the bank were good protection. Even the sage grew
tall enough to hide a man.

The tired horses of the soldiers were frightened. Some broke away and ran toward the river, where the Cheyenne women caught and led them back to their own pony herd. The braves under Gall sought out the soldiers assigned the task of holding the horses of their comrades fighting on foot. The horse handlers had led the mounts up into the shelter of the ravines, but Sioux guns killed the men, picking them off carefully as a hunter does game. Then, with waving blankets and loud shouts, the braves drove the horses down to the waiting Cheyenne women. Each captured horse was worth double: the animal itself, and the filled saddlebags, heavy with the reserve ammunition of the soldiers.

When the smoke of the original charge had thinned, the Indians crept forward again. They could see that the soldiers had parted into three groups. One group was on the left, another on the right, with the greatest number still in the center.

Again the air was filled, not with smoke but with the dust raised by the Sioux and Cheyenne ponies. It rose in a great ring all around an ever-tightening circle, and in the middle were the soldiers. The sound of bullets was like the humming of bees, and the swirling dust was like water eddying about a stone. As long as they had powder, the Indians used their guns. When it was gone they shot arrows, aiming them high so that they would fall into the massed troops in the center.

On the higher ground where the Oglala and the Miniconjou were fighting, soldiers and horses fell alike. Living soldiers used their dead mounts as breastwork, firing over them, but it was no protection against the rain of arrows falling from the sky. Some of the men broke away and tried to make a dash down the slope, but always they were seen and pursued by a vengeful band of Sioux. None was permitted to escape.

Two Moon's Cheyenne advanced cautiously up the left side of the slope. Here the white soldiers were fighting on foot. Only their officer had retained his horse, and he rode up and down the line, shouting to his men and firing his hand gun at the Cheyenne. When there was no more ammunition in his belt, he threw the gun away and fought with a knife, leaning from horseback to thrust at the advancing Indians.

Even at a time like this, Two Moon admired the white officer's courage. He was a brave man, wearing a buckskin shirt, with black hair on his head and on his upper lip. His horse was a fine sorrel with a white face and four white legs.

But he had to die. They all had to die. They had to be driven from the land forever.

At last it was finished, and it seemed a little strange to think upon. A short while ago there were more than two hundred soldiers here. Now, in the time it took the sun to travel the length of a lodge pole, not one was alive.

The Indians went among the dead, stripping them of their clothes and taking the scalps of those who had hair enough to dangle from a belt or lodge pole. But when they came to the man who had ridden the sorrel horse, Two Moon would let no one take his black hair or his buckskin jacket.

"He was a brave man," he told the others, "the bravest in the battle."

And because Two Moon was a chief, his words had meaning, and the warriors left the man alone.

There was another there who some said was the great chief, Long Hair. Two Moon had never seen him, so he did not know. This man's hair was neither long nor yellow but the color of grass after the frost, and the Indians did not take it, for it was too short. But they counted coup on his dead body. Four men touched him with long coup sticks where he lay, and of these, Two Moon was the fourth.

The white chief was in the great pile of slain at the top of the hill, a bullet wound in his temple and another in his chest. He had not feared death, for he was smiling.

Perhaps it was Long Hair, agreed Two Moon, but he was not the bravest man there. The bravest had been the stranger on the sorrel horse.

Most of the horses remaining on the hill were dead, and the few living were so weary that they stood, waiting to be caught. They were not even afraid of the Indians as the horses of the white soldiers generally were. The young braves who took them looked them over first for wounds. If a horse was bleeding badly, it was left behind.

When it was made certain all those in the army that had come seeking a battle with the Sioux were dead, the warriors left the field. Most of them returned to dispatch the soldiers still on the hill beyond the Hunkpapa camp. It would be easier this time, they told each other. Because of the captured saddlebags, they now had plenty of ammunition.

3:30 p.m.—12 a.m.

Bugler Martin rode as fast as his tired horse would go. It was not an uneventful trip.

Almost immediately after leaving the battalion he met a rider, also urging his mount to a gallop. It was Boston Custer, the general's younger brother, who had accompanied the column in the civilian capacity of packer. The fact that General Custer had managed to include two members of his own family on the expedition had resulted in no little criticism on the part of some of the officers and troops. Bugler Martin did not share their view. Neither Captain Tom Custer nor Boston had singled him out as a target for their jokes.

"Where's the general?" shouted Boston, not even checking his horse to receive a reply.

Martin pointed over his shoulder toward the

ravine, and young Custer spurred his horse in a frantic effort to overtake the troops.

As he rode on, Martin wondered how he was expected to find Benteen. No one had told him where to look. Lieutenant Cooke had merely said to ride back over the route they had taken. Perhaps by this time Company H would have fulfilled their mission, whatever it was, and would be following the trail.

When he approached the knoll where he and Custer had observed the Indian encampment, he decided it was worth the extra time to ride to the top. The summit gave a good view of part of the valley, and perhaps he could see Benteen's battalion.

As his horse stumbled up the slope, Martin thought he could hear gunfire. It grew louder as he ascended, and when he reached the top, he could see Reno's detachment in the valley below. They were in a skirmish line, and riding around and around them were hundreds of Indians.

For a moment Martin could only stare. It had been no more than fifteen minutes since he and General Custer had looked down into that valley, and at that time not a warrior was in sight. Now they sprung up like toadstools after a rain.

He did not have time to watch. His message was

for Benteen, and there was no sign of the captain's three companies in the valley. Martin could only obey orders, go back to the trail, and continue on.

As he wheeled his horse, he heard firing close at hand. There were Indians on this side of the river, too. They had been lying in ambush and now were firing at him. He dug his cavalry spurs into the white horse, and as four or five bullets zipped around him, he galloped back down the slope.

Obviously it was but one small party, for the firing did not continue, but it was a hot day and growing more uncomfortable by the minute. Bugler Martin wished he were any place but here.

The white horse was going slower and slower. Even the spurs were useless now, for the animal had almost spent its last strength. Martin wondered if he would have to continue on foot.

Then he saw the cloud of approaching dust. A few moments later he recognized a familiar burly figure on a blood bay, riding a little in advance of the cloud. It was his captain, Captain Benteen, with his own orderly bugler close behind.

Martin waved his hat in excitement. Once more he tried to urge his mount forward, but the white horse stood still, his head low, his body trembling with exhaustion.

The captain arrived at a fast trot. Martin saluted and handed him the note from Lieutenant Cooke. Just to make sure, he gave him the general's verbal message, too. It was a big encampment. The captain was to hurry and bring the packs.

Benteen read the message and handed it to Captain Weir who, by this time, had ridden up with the troops.

"What's the matter with your horse, Orderly?" The cavalryman's eyes looked critically at Martin's trembling mount.

"Just tired out, I guess, sir."

"Tired out? Look at his hip," ordered the captain, frowning. "You're lucky it wasn't you."

Martin turned in the saddle. The white flank was stained red. One of the Indian bullets had found its mark in the bandsman's horse. He slid to the ground hastily. It had been a good horse after all, better than he had thought.

The packtrain was not far behind. It was in sight, perhaps a mile away, and the mules were coming along well today. Benteen did not wait. He continued ahead with his own companies, following the trail taken by Custer and his men.

Before long they could hear the unmistakable sounds of gunfire, which grew louder as they advanced. Benteen gave orders to draw pistols, and led his men on at a gallop. For the hundredth time he chafed at the orders that had sent him riding off on a fool's errand. There had been no Sioux in the south, nothing but ridge after empty ridge studded with juniper and sage. He had followed his orders to the letter and explored the first two. Then he had led his men back to the trail to rejoin the regiment. And high time, too. From the sounds of things there were two battles going on simultaneously: one on the bluffs, another some distance ahead.

As they neared the spot where Major Reno's battalion had turned off to make the crossing of the Little Big Horn, they encountered a small group of Ree scouts who were driving off a few captured Sioux ponies. Benteen halted his command to speak with them.

They shouted, *"Otoe Sioux,* many Sioux!" as they rode by, herding their prizes toward the safety of the Wolf Mountains.

There was no interpreter, but Benteen did not need one. There were "many Sioux" on the bluffs, and this battle was the nearest to hand. He led his three companies toward the river, and found Reno's command reassembling on a hilltop just beyond the first ridge.

The major saw them coming and hurried to meet them on foot. He had lost his hat and had a handkerchief tied around his head.

"But God's sake, Benteen, halt your command and help me," he cried. "I've lost half my men."

Part of his troops were still coming up the slope, some mounted and some on foot. A few were

struggling in the river bottom, having been left behind in the woods. Most were excited and demoralized, but one veteran strode jauntily along, disregarding the Indian snipers from nearby hillsides, waving a fresh scalp.

Benteen took temporary command. He ordered his own men to divide their ammunition with Reno's forces, and laid out hasty defense lines on the summit of the hill. He asked the whereabouts of Custer, but the dazed major did not know. The general was supposed to have supported Reno's attack on the village, but there had been no sign of him.

Benteen reported the second battle he had heard in progress farther down the valley. They could hear firing in the distance and concluded that the general, with his five companies, was soundly whipping the Sioux.

Reno's losses had been tremendous. A third of his battalion had been killed or wounded. He was especially unnerved by the death of Bloody Knife, who had been shot so close by that his blood had gushed over the major's coat. Lonesome Charley Reynolds had been killed, too, just as he had foretold would happen, also the interpreter Dorman and three officers, including the surgeon, Dr. De-Wolfe.

Since the arrival of Benteen's troops, the Indians' fire had fallen off. Now only a few snipers remained to harass the soldiers. In the valley to the west the gunfire still continued.

Everyone agreed that the second battle must be Custer's, and without orders Captain Weir with D Company, followed moments later by Benteen and companies H, K, and M, marched downstream to get what Benteen called "the lay of the land." They waited on a high point of the bluffs for Reno's column to catch up, and Benteen set up a guidon on the crest to show Custer the location of the command should he arrive first. They could see Indians in the valley and a pony herd, but no trace of the general's battalion. By now the sounds of battle in the valley had died away.

Major Reno, somewhat recovered by this time, insisted on awaiting the arrival of the packtrain, then the remaining companies started downriver. By the time they caught up with Benteen's men, Indians by the thousands began pouring out of the valley, all headed in their direction. The odds were too great. They had to retreat.

None of the hilltops was well suited for defense, but the one to which Reno had first led his troops was the best. This time there was no frenzied rout. The battalion made an orderly retreat. They even had time to herd the mules and horses into a swale and to place the wounded in the most protected spots before the Sioux were upon them.

The Indians attacked from every side, and because their medicine was strong, each warrior fought without fear for his own safety. The crest of the hill was shaped like a saucer, and the troopers lay flat on the ground, their only protection the saddles or packs they had stacked before them. There were no arrows used. This time the Indians had guns and amunition to match the whites, and in the three hours of battle the casualties increased.

Then abruptly the battle ceased.

Troopers new to Indian warfare, and there were many of these, looked to the veterans for explanation. The Sioux had returned to their encampment, they were told. Indians did not fight during the hours of darkness.

In the smoke-filled air the sun had appeared, a glowing ball of fire as it dipped below the mountains in the west, and almost at once the quick Montana twilight settled. There was no moon, and before long the chill of the high plains sent each trooper searching for his army greatcoat tied to the cantle of his saddle.

Through the long night a red reflection in the sky told of council fires in the Sioux encampment.

There was the constant throb of tomtoms, once a sudden burst of gunfire, and occasionally the wind carried the high-pitched chanting of Indian voices.

"Scalp dances!" the troopers told each other bitterly. "The dirty redskins are holding scalp dances."

There was not much time to dwell on that, however. There was too much to be done: trenches to dig, breastworks of dead horses and saddles to heap up, for they knew the enemy would return at first light.

There were only a few spades and axes in the packs, and after these had been doled out, the men dug in the porous soil with cups and tin mess kits, even their bare hands.

While they worked, they spoke of the one thing on every mind. Where was Custer? He had ordered them to attack, promising support, and then abandoned them. Perhaps he had been repulsed and started downstream to join Terry and Gibbon's forces by a roundabout route. But the majority agreed that Custer's men had been surrounded, just as they themselves were now, and that they would all have to wait the arrival of the infantry before they could escape.

JUNE 26, 1876

1

Morning came early. By two thirty streaks of pink and yellow stained the eastern sky, and the valley below crept out of blackness into a gray mist. All but the guard had dropped into exhausted sleep, but at the sound of two signal shots every trooper was awake.

Again they were surrounded by Sioux and Cheyenne, who lay hidden behind rough hummocks on the slope or had taken shelter in the innumerable coulees and ravines that ran down the sides. Some had climbed to the top of a small hill which was slightly higher than the one chosen for defense, from which they could pour bullets into the regiment's southern line.

The preceding night each company had been assigned a definite place in the line. Captain Benteen's Company H held the key position on the bluff. Company B, under McDougall, occupied the opposite and shorter side, facing the Indian encampment, with Moylan's men spread across the swale, protecting the corral. The others had been assigned posts in between, but Company H, in holding the southern ridge by itself, occupied almost as much line as the others combined.

The attack was heavy and continuous from all sides, with the troopers returning the fire as best they could. In each company at least one man was assigned the task of extracting jammed cartridges, and in Company M Lieutenant French took on the thankless job himself. He squatted on the ground beside his men, forcing out with a knife the shell that had jammed in the carbine barrel. Then he reloaded, and as he passed it back to its owner, he reached for a second faulty rifle with his other hand.

The Indians tried to draw fire by standing erect for a moment or by raising arrows over the top of ravines, but the men were forbidden to waste shells on such tricks. When they withheld their fire for several minutes, a small war party made a rushing charge upon the lines. That was the time to fire, when there were many advancing targets.

But for every Indian who fell, there were many to take his place. There were so many eager warriors, anxious to take part in the battle, that there was not room for them all on the hill. A thousand stood watching, awaiting a turn, below on the river bottom, and as many more occupied the nearby bluffs out of range. The troopers could not understand why with so many fighters the Indians did not make one great advance, overpowering with their numbers.

Company H exposed to the fire of the Sioux on the higher bluff suffered more than most. This was the thinnest point in the line, and the Indians realized it and concentrated upon it. But the morale of Benteen's men was good. Unlike the others, they had had a little sleep. There had been too few spades and digging equipment the night before. The supply was exhausted before Company H received any. When Captain Benteen saw his men digging futilely with their bare hands, he had told them to stop and wrap up in their blankets as protection against the light rain that was falling. They were already exhausted, and the rest was important, too. Now their only breastwork was the small pile of saddles and such boxes as they could secure from the packtrain.

Benteen walked up and down the line, his white hair shining in the morning sun, smiling and speaking encouragingly to his men.

"You'd better watch out for yourself, sir." Trooper Charley Windolph voiced the feeling of all the men. The captain was making a fine target of himself.

"Don't you worry about me. I'll be all right," Benteen assured him staunchly.

But he was fearful for his men, the thinness of the line, and the steadily mounting number of injuries. He went to Reno, demanding reinforcements, and the major reluctantly gave him Lieutenant French and M Company.

It made a big difference. With a company of reinforcements, Benteen decided to try to get a little water for the relief of the regiment.

The problem of water had been growing increasingly more serious. Some had full canteens in the beginning, but those were empty now. From the semiprotected spot where the wounded lay came a constant moaning and the sound of weak voices crying out for water. Even the uninjured troopers were suffering. Their throats were parched, their tongues swollen, and as one of them said, "That sun is cooking the blood in my veins."

A few yards directly in front of Benteen's position a small ravine headed down to the river some six hundred yards below. It was filled with Indians, but the captain led a charge down the slope and drove them out. Surprised at the sudden advance, the Sioux scattered while not a trooper was harmed.

Now came the dangerous part. From the end of the ravine it was necessary to go thirty feet over open country to reach the river. During that time the water carriers would be exposed to fire from the opposite bank. It was a risky proceeding, too hazardous to be undertaken under orders, so Benteen called for volunteers. They were not slow in coming, and he took the first seventeen to step forward. For protection he chose the four best shots in H Company: Sergeant George Geiger, Blacksmith Henry Meckling, Saddler Otto Voit, and Trooper Charley Windolph.

Loaded with all the available cooking pots and canteens, the volunteers dashed across the open space to throw themselves flat beside the bank. Behind them, in the open, stood the four sharpshooters, who kept up a steady fire, picking their targets skillfully. In spite of their efforts, one water carrier was killed and half a dozen injured.

Soon after noon the firing ceased. All the Sioux converged across the river, where a scout had ridden in from the village.

During the lull, Benteen secured the small supply of shovels and set his men to throwing up breastworks along his line. Some of the others crept to the river and refilled the already emptied receptacles with water. No one else left his position. The officers feared a trick, and vigilance was not relaxed.

In a short time the Indians returned to their former positions, but it was not as it had been before. Now there were no onlookers in the river bottom or on the bluffs, nor was the firing quite so concentrated. It fell away, little by little, area after area, until only a scattering of the enemy remained in key positions.

Major Reno prepared a dispatch for General Terry, telling him of their position and what had happened. He stated that he had no knowledge of Custer. The scouts to whom he tried to entrust the copies refused to go at first, but finally they agreed. They were soon back with the news that the valley was too full of Sioux. They could not get through.

Major Reno's opinion of Indian scouts sank even lower. He refused to change it even after Lieutenant Varnum tried to tell him of the valor of the Crow scouts in the fighting line.

Three Crows had joined the troops last night under cover of darkness. They had been prohibited by Mitch Bouyer from following Custer, but the prospect of fighting Sioux was too enticing, and they had stopped off here. Originally there had been four of them, but one of their number, Curly, had hidden on the bluffs to watch Custer's charge, and the others had gone on without him.

The three had taken a place in the line beside Knife Face Varnum, and the troopers agreed that they had fought as hard as anyone. One of them, White Swan, had continued fighting even after he was severely wounded, but still Major Reno had no praise. Crow, Ree, Sioux—they were all Indians, and were not to be trusted.

Across the river, smoke began drifting south. The scouts said that the Sioux had fired the grass, which was strange unless they were preparing to leave. By this time the shots of the snipers had stopped entirely, and the troopers went to the brow of the hill to watch.

From time to time, the wind blew the heavy smoke away, and when that happened, they could glimpse thousands of Indians, warriors on their ponies, dressed in fighting regalia, women and children, heavily loaded travois, scampering dogs, and closely herded ponies. The smoke would close over like a rolling screen, but when it opened again, there would be the procession, headed south.

Again the officers feared a trick. The Sioux might be sending away only their women and children with enough warriors for protection. The greatest number might still be lying in wait. The troopers stayed where they were, watching.

The moving community took several hours to pass from view, but it was gone by dusk. The guards led the remaining horses and mules down to the river, then put them out to graze. The animals had neither eaten nor drunk since yesterday.

In silence that was almost as terrifying as the noise of battle, the soldiers buried their dead in the shallow trenches that had been dug to protect the living, and the regiment moved down off the hill, closer to water.

The cooks had prepared the only supper they could, coffee and hardtack soaked in water, but to men who had been without food for thirty-six hours it was the best meal they had ever eaten. A guard was posted, and the others gratefully lay on the hard ground. They were all too exhausted to remember the pressing question which had concerned them the night before: Where was Custer?

2

Sitting Bull had spent the hours of yesterday's battle in his lodge, making medicine and praying to *Wakan Tanka* for victory. The sun had set and darkness covered the encampment before he came out. By that time the warriors had returned, bringing their dead and wounded.

There were no scalp dances that night, for too many Sioux and Cheyenne had been lost in battle. It would have been discourteous to those who had lost a father or a son to celebrate the victory then. The camps were filled with drumming and the keening of those who for four days would mourn their dead. Some of the young agency bucks found fiery water in the canteens of the soldiers, and the drinking took away their senses. They fired their new rifles at the stars, but the *akicita* (warriors chosen to keep order) soon put an end to that.

Now this morning when the warriors were to return to the hill to kill more white soldiers, Sitting Bull advised caution. Much of their medicine had been spent in yesterday's battle. It was no longer strong enough for a mass attack. Too many brave young men would be killed.

In this, Crazy Horse concurred. He reminded them that there was no water on the hill. If the warriors would content themselves with holding the soldiers there, thirst and the sun would drive them to the river. There they could be killed with little loss to the Sioux and Cheyenne.

After the warriors left, Sitting Bull went with the Big Bellies to the battlefield near Medicine Tail Coulee to count the dead.

One man carried a bundle of small sticks, and when they came to a dead man, he handed one of the sticks to a second man. There had been thirty-nine bodies of slain Sioux upon the field yesterday, and seven Cheyenne, but sixty wounded warriors had been carried into camp. As for the slain white soldiers, the sticks to exchange hands numbered over two hundred.

The war women (those women who delighted in following warriors to the field once the battle was ended) had been here with their knives. Some

of the bodies were badly mutilated. All of them were stripped of clothing, and most of them scalped.

Sitting Bull was angry when he saw them. Not at the scalping, for that was a badge of honor, a ritualistic necessity for men who believed the human spirit was in the human hair, but he frowned at the sight of bodies stripped of clothing.

"The dead soldiers were the gift of *Wakan Tanka*," he declared. "It was our right to kill them, but not our right to take their possessions. The Sioux should not have touched the spoils. When

they set their hearts upon the goods of the white man, it will prove a curse to our nation."

The others were silent. Sitting Bull had given this warning before, at the time of his vision, and all had heard. But it was impossible to hold back young warriors with their blood still hot from fighting, and what clothing and personal belongings they had left behind, the war women had taken as their due.

They stood at the top of the hill where lay the greatest number of soldiers. One of them asked if that was truly Long Hair lying there. Sitting Bull did not know. Like Two Moon, he had never seen the man before.

"But he was a brave man," he insisted. "All these men were as good as ever fought. When they rode up, their horses were tired and they were tired. When they got off their horses, they could not stand firmly on their feet. They swayed to and fro—so my young men told me—like the limbs of cypresses in a great wind. Some of them staggered under their guns. They began to fight at once, but our camps were aroused, and there were plenty of our warriors to meet them. There were brave men on both sides, mighty fighters. The white soldiers came here seeking this fight. The Sioux and Cheyenne but defended themselves."

When the sun was overhead, a small group of Sioux rode up the Greasy Grass. They had been hunting and were too late for the battle, but they brought news.

Many white soldiers were coming, an army of walking soldiers. Doubtless they would stop for darkness, but the next sun would see them at the encampment.

Sitting Bull gave orders, and the women began dismantling the lodges and gathering up their possessions.

The mourners hurried to prepare their dead.

The slain Sioux and Cheyenne were dressed in their finest shirts and leggings, with earrings of dentalium shells and quilled amulets on their arms. Their faces were painted red, and eagle feathers placed in their hair. Each warrior was wrapped in a blanket, and his weapons, pots of war paint, and his flute placed next to him on a scaffold made of four forked poles. Then a painted tepee was set above the scaffold, and the opening sewed up. This much only could they do for their dead. They dared not stay to mourn the full allotted time.

While this was going on, a messenger had been sent to Crazy Horse, who then called together all the warriors at the hill. It would not do to let the soldiers know that the Indians were moving on, for they might gain courage and pursue too soon. The retreat must be made in a gradual manner. The fighting would be resumed, and the braves would leave a few score at a time. Then, when the moving procession was well underway, the last of the warriors would quit the hill and overtake the others.

"Ai," said the Hunkpapa, the Oglala, the Miniconjou, and the other Sioux.

"Hoh," said Two Moon's people in their soft Cheyenne.

All understood and agreed. And so it was done.

The women made short work of dismantling their lodges, fastening one end of the poles to a pony and allowing the other ends to drag behind, rolling the buffalo-hide cover into a bundle, securing the dried meat and vegetables, the cooking utensils, and the household belongings into packs for the travois.

Those who had lost a husband in the battle had little to carry, for the household goods of a slain warrior were left behind. His family must start building anew. Then the unridden ponies were herded in from the grasslands, and the caravan was underway.

As guests, the Cheyenne had the place of honor in the lead. The people of Sitting Bull, the Hunkpapa, brought up the rear, for they were hosts. And in between came all the other tribes of the seven council fires. It was a great procession, extending over the space of three miles in length and a half mile in width.

The warriors from the hill joined their own tribes in small groups, but before they left, they fired the prairies, partly to cover their retreat and partly to destroy the remaining grass which could give food to the horses of the enemy.

Southward they moved, toward the vastness of the White Rain Mountains, called by the whites the Big Horns. They were the victors of a battle with soldiers who had come falling into their camp, just as *Wakan Tanka* foretold.

JUNE 27, 1876

Newly appointed sergeant, Charley Windolph stood with the enlisted men watching the slow moving dust trail across the river. A short distance away were the officers of Reno's command, watching the same dust and wondering the same thing. Who was making it? Indians returning to resume the battle? Or reinforcements?

Up until nine thirty it had been a tedious morning. There had been reveille without guns. The horses had been cared for, and breakfast eaten. The menu was the same as last night's supper, soaked hardtack and coffee, but today it was received with a few grumbles.

There had been congratulations for Charley Windolph. Many of the men in H Company had not realized that he had been made a sergeant yesterday. Captain Benteen had promoted him on the battlefield. One sergeant and two men from Company H had been killed, and twelve wounded. The captain said Charley had earned the promotion.

There was not an Indian to be seen across the river, only a few bare lodge poles, with a grazing pony or two. Nevertheless Major Reno still believed this might be a trick. He ordered his men to hold themselves in readiness.

When the dust trail was sighted, some of them agreed the major could be right. Assembly was sounded; the horses placed in a protected position; and all kettles and canteens filled with water. Rifle pits had already been dug, so there was nothing to do now but wait.

The dust moved slowly, too slowly for Indian ponies, so everyone agreed it had to be reinforcements. But whose command? It couldn't be Custer. The officers with field glasses had announced that there were no gray horses, and Custer had a full company of grays. Perhaps it was Gibbon's infantry under General Terry. Or General Crook. Although Crook should have been coming from the south, he won the vote. The troopers gave him three cheers on the spot.

Most of them had been so intent on the approaching dust that they had not noticed two riders ford the first crossing above the old Sioux encampment. The bugler sounded attention as the men started riding up the coulee, and every trooper stiffened.

The first man wore a buckskin jacket, but he was followed by a second wearing army blue. Both faces under their brimmed hats were reassuringly white.

When they arrived, the leader flung himself from his horse and asked for Lieutenant Godfrey.

Charley Windolph decided the two must be old friends, for Godfrey rushed forward, greeting the other warmly and calling him, "Bradley." A whisper ran round the circle of troopers that this was Lieutenant Bradley, chief of scouts for Gibbon's infantry.

"Where is Custer?" Lieutenant Godfrey voiced the question in everyone's mind, and they all held their breaths awaiting the answer.

"I don't know, but I suppose he has been killed. We counted 197 dead bodies. I don't suppose anybody escaped."

In the great unbelieving silence, Bradley went on to tell his story. A Crow scout named Curly had reported at the junction of the Little Big Horn and the Big Horn rivers yesterday. There had been no interpreter present, but he made them understand that there had been a battle in which all the white soldiers had been slain. Of course no one believed him, but at dawn Bradley started out to search. Surprisingly the Crow had been right. Bradley had found the battlefield strewn with dead bodies, and he was certain no one had escaped. Although he had counted only 197, there were other bodies near the river and scattered through the brush which would have to be searched out.

The troopers looked at each other with disbelief. Never before had such a thing happened. It couldn't have happened—not a whole battalion, particularly not Custer's.

Shortly afterward, General Terry arrived with a group of officers on horseback. The infantry followed more slowly, but it would be there by afternoon. He went into immediate conference with Major Reno's staff while the troopers waited, talking in low voices about this terrible thing. It was hard to realize, and many still refused to believe it. Surely there must be some survivors.

The officers thought so, too, and detachments were sent out to search for anyone who might be in hiding. Captain Benteen, with Captain Weir,

Lieutenant Varnum, and fourteen troopers, was ordered to follow Custer's trail and try to determine how the battle had been fought. Sergeant Windolph was one of the fourteen.

They followed along the crest of the bluffs behind their present camp for perhaps three miles before arriving at a ravine that led down to the river. It was deep, and the bottom was cut up into smaller ravines and by the marks left by the shod feet of many horses. A little farther on, they found what they were seeking.

It was hard to determine exactly what had taken place. Obviously the Indian attack had been sudden and ferocious, and Custer's command had little chance to form battle lines. As Captain Benteen said, "Someone could scatter a handful of corn on the field and get as close a resemblance to lines as this." He believed that an attempt at a stand had been made on the hill itself, but bodies were found over an area of ten acres.

On the south slope they found the bodies of Lieutenant Calhoun's L Company, and on the north those of Captain Keogh's I. The men of the Wild I had died in a group, as if they might have been trying to form a skirmish line.

Behind a hastily improvised barricade of dead

horses on the summit of the hill were the remains of C, F, and E companies. General Custer was there, surrounded by his men.

The bodies had been stripped, most of them scalped, and some mutilated almost beyond recognition. Sergeant Windolph's stomach churned, and he felt sorry for the men in the burial squad who at General Terry's orders were now arriving on the field.

As Lieutenant Bradley had said there was no human survivor, but in the bushes near the river, someone found Captain Keogh's horse, Comanche.

With six bullet wounds, it had been passed over by the Cheyenne women, but the troopers brought it back, and the dun-colored horse lived to become the pampered mascot of the Seventh Cavalry.

On their return they passed through the former tribal encampment of the Indians. A company of Gibbon's infantry was there, smashing the household goods of the dead warriors so that they would be useless to any returning Indians.

The burial lodges had been set ablaze, but first they must have cut the stitches and removed the wrapping blankets from the warriors. One soldier had an eagle feather in his army cap. Others wore dentalium earrings and quilled amulets on their wrists.

Captain Benteen did not halt, but continued on to camp. They had seen enough of Indians for a while. Of the 585 men and 31 officers who had started out with the Seventh Cavalry, 265 were dead; 31, all from Reno's command, were seriously wounded. All they asked now was to mount up and ride home.

Suggested Further Reading

BLEEKER, SONIA E., *The Sioux Indians*. Morrow, New York: 1962.

GARST, SHANNON, *Crazy Horse*. Houghton Mifflin, Cambridge, Massachusetts: 1950.

HOFSINDE, ROBERT, *Indian Warriors and Their Weapons*. Morrow, New York: 1965.

LEIGHTON, MARGARET, *Comanche of the Seventh*. Farrar, Straus and Giroux, New York: 1957.

PLACE, MARIAN T., *Buckskins and Buffalo*. Holt, Rinehart and Winston, New York: 1964.

RANDALL, RUTH P., *I, Elizabeth*. Little, Brown, Boston, Massachusetts: 1966.

Bibliography

GRAHAM, COL. WILLIAM A., Judge Advocate U.S. Army Retired, *The Custer Myth*. Stackpole, Harrisburg, Pennsylvania: 1953.

———, *The Story of the Little Bighorn*. Stackpole, Harrisburg, Pennsylvania: 1957.

HASSRICK, ROYAL B., *The Sioux*. University of Oklahoma Press, Norman, Oklahoma: 1964.

HUNT, FRAZIER, *I Fought With Custer*. Scribner's, New York: 1947.

KINSLEY, D. A., *Favor the Bold*. Holt, Rinehart and Winston, New York: 1968.

MILNER, JOE E. and E. R. FORREST, *California Joe, with an Authentic Account of Custer's Last Fight* by William H. C. Bowen. Caxton Printers, Caldwell, Idaho: 1935.

SANDOZ, MARI, *Crazy Horse*. Knopf, New York: 1942.

STEWART, EDGAR I., *Custer's Luck*. University of Oklahoma Press, Norman, Oklahoma: 1955.

VESTAL, STANLEY, *Sitting Bull*. University of Oklahoma Press, Norman, Oklahoma: 1957.

Index

About the Author

Evelyn Sibley Lampman has a natural interest in the story of the American West. Her great-grandparents went out West in a covered wagon as pioneers. Her father was a small-town lawyer, and her mother a schoolteacher there. Mrs. Lampman was born and raised in a small Oregon town, close to an Indian reservation. She studied at Oregon State College and, in fact, still lives in Oregon.

Evelyn Sibley Lampman has always been a writer. She has well over thirty books to her credit and many honors, including the Dorothy Canfield Fisher Award, and the Western Writers Spur Award. Once she was even chosen to be grand marshal in a local Santa Claus parade and this, she writes, was "the most fun of all."

About the Illustrator

John Gretzer was born in Council Bluffs, Iowa, attended the University of Omaha, and spent one year at the Kansas City Art Institute, studying under Thomas Hart Benton.

Mr. Gretzer has been active in the production of animated movies and in department-store advertising. He was at one time art director for a publishing firm and now undertakes freelance asignments involving advertising and editorial art. He is the illustrator of several books for children.

Mr. Gretzer and his family live in Perkasie, Pennsylvania.